Requiem for a Rebel

by
Hugh Gorman

ISBN: 0-8341-0652-3

Hugh Gorman
323, 223 Tuscany Springs Blvd.
Calgary, Alberta T3L 2M2

Dedication

To
Joan, my constant helpmeet,
and
Wes and Tim, my two sons,
Daily reminders of God's great love

Contents

Obituary of a Rebel

Memories of Hugh Gorman

"There was just no hope for him . . . I wanted nothing to do with him; for when he was sober, he'd be conning someone to get money for a drink; and when he was drunk, he was just raving mad. I thought he'd end up in jail again . . . or in Purdysburn Asylum . . . or in the city cemetery."

—David Gorman, father

"Even when Hugh was bubbling with charm and humor, you never knew when he'd erupt like a volcano. One minute he was so refined, and the next he could be like a wild animal."

—Ann Gorman, sister

"Hugh Gorman was a no-good scoundrel."

—Rev. James Macleod, Dromore, Ireland

"Lonely women must be guarded at night, and the public must be protected from this man."

—Judge Porter, Belfast City Commission

"Since coming here, he's done nothing but intimidate and bully the other prisoners."

—Prison officer, Belfast

"Hugh Gorman: Military conduct—indifferent. Cause for discharge—misconduct. Attempt at reenlistment renders this man liable to imprisonment for two years."
—Official British Army Records

"hugh had great ideas about how he was going to live,
but he started in on great drinking sprees. he
stole money, robbed stores and people.
he terrorized . . . and caused ugly scenes
in the streets of belfast."
—Ann Kiemel, in *It's Incredible*,
Tyndale House Publishers

"Here was a young man who dipped deeply into the golden honey jar of life's amazing, but evanescent joys. At the age of 17, there were few evil experiences he did not know."
—C. L. J., *Christian Herald*, England

1

God Can . . . !

What was going on among the inmates of Belfast Prison? What was the message being whispered from cell to cell? Why was there an enthusiasm at large that was alien to any penal institution?

In the prison visiting room, Joe McAllister was being visited by his wife, Lily. They sat in silence just looking at each other, and touching fingers through the wire grill, until the officer walked away. Lily moved her chair closer and whispered, "Hughie Gorman will be coming in today."

When Joe got back to his work in the prison kitchen, the news spread. A trusty from each wing heard it when they picked up the noon meal; and as they served it from cell to cell, the news spread to every part of the prison. Before I got there in the afternoon, many were anticipating my arrival.

It was with mixed feelings I approached the huge

prison gates on the Crumlin Road, conscious of the two men, one on either side of me. I remembered the last time I entered the prison. It was through the underground tunnel from the courthouse across the road. The guards at the gate sprang to attention and saluted but kept staring at me as if they wanted to speak. I smiled and nodded in greeting.

The old familiar sounds were all there: the rattling of keys, clanging of gates, slamming of cell doors, clippety-clopping of prison-made boots on the highly polished tile floor; and all of these noises echoing and reechoing along the corridors. The place hadn't changed much; and although there were a few new officers, most of them were "old hands" who'd been there for years. In their smartly tailored and pressed uniforms, one could detect their military background; and except for the bunch of keys and the riot sticks concealed inside their right pant leg, they were all very much like soldiers.

Upon entering the administration building, we were informed that the special service was about to start in the prison chapel, to which we were escorted by one of the officers. There was a different atmosphere in the chapel—less prison like—and one was immediately conscious of the hubbub as the prisoners conversed in whispers. Looking around at the sea of faces, I recognized scores of the men. Many were my personal friends, others were army buddies, while some had been my companions as we walked and talked in the prison exercise yard. I acknowledged the smiles of recogniton.

Bill Hoyt, a sharply dressed, handsome young song evangelist, was leading the singing; and how he really got those guys singing as they had never sung before! They were thrilled as they listened to Bill sing his package of special sacred songs, enjoying it so much they applauded for more. After singing an extra number, Bill introduced

Dr. Larry Love, the dynamic Canadian preacher, who at that time was an associate evangelist with the Billy Graham Evangelistic Association. He was conducting a city-wide crusade in the King's Hall every night, and in the afternoons in the prison chapel.

"In the past two days you've been listening to me preach," said Dr. Love. "Today we're going to have a change, for I've taken the liberty to invite a guest speaker, and he's no stranger to many of you. He's certainly no stranger to this prison, for at one time he sat where you're sitting now. Men, our preacher today is one of your own friends from this city, the Rev. Hugh Gorman."

As I walked to the pulpit, those guys whistled, stamped their feet, and clapped their hands; and some shouted, "Good old Gormey!" The officers paced nervously up and down the aisles, wondering what it was all about, and what they should do; but the prisoners settled down when I raised my hands for silence.

"Hey, you guys," I joked, "wha'cha kickin' up a racket for? D'ya wanna go back t'yer cells? . . . or to sewing mailbags?"

"Will you come and help us?" shouted a prisoner whose voice I recognized.

"Ah, I see wee Bobbie there in his usual pew. I was in court when his ma pleaded with the beak:

> "Don't sent my Bob to prison;
> He wasn't one to roam.
> He didn't steal those chickens;
> They all followed him home."

They all had a good laugh, and I laughed with them; but in my heart I sobbed for every one of those men, knowing that many of them had the cards stacked against them from the day they were born. I honestly longed for them to have the same chance I had to know Christ and what it means to be free indeed.

11

"You know, men," I continued, "the last time I got out of this joint, as I was walking out through the gate, the screw said to me, 'Why don't you leave your gear here, Gorman? You'll be back soon anyhow.' I should've been back a long time ago; and I should be sitting down there with you guys. I would've been here sooner, and almost was, but something happened to me. As I came out of the Loyola bar in Sandy Row one Saturday night, a preacher by the name of Bert Kelly grabbed me by the arm and challenged me with these words, 'Gorman, God can change your life!' "

A lot had happened since that night, but I'll never forget the encounter I had with Bert Kelly, for it was my first encounter with God. I can remember it as if it were yesterday. . . .

Saturday. I had to look at the morning paper to see what day it was! And Saturdays were always the same around our house, as things got off to a slow start because no one had to work. Everybody slept late, and then after brunch each member of the family followed their own individual pursuits, for we were not a "play together" or "stay together" family. Mother went to do her weekend shopping, which gave her an opportunity to visit with friends. Father settled down to watch the world of sports on the shilling-in-the-slot television. Three of my brothers spent their time between the bar and the bookies. My sister usually had a date which kept her out most of the day. And my youngest brother was still at the stage where Saturday wasn't complete without a visit to the matinee at the Sandro Cinema, or the "Ranch" as it was called.

I was sick with an awful hangover, not knowing how I'd come home the night before, or what I'd been doing for the past two days. No one spoke to me when I came downstairs, and I'd the feeling that something was wrong, but didn't dare ask what it was. With that kind of atmosphere, I wanted to get away to the bar as soon as possible.

As I ate breakfast, someone opened the front door; sounds came in from the street—a child's voice, a woman calling, traffic passing on the Donegall Road. I hurriedly ate, got washed, shaved, and got ready to go.

Mrs. Moore, our next-door neighbor, was sweeping the sidewalk in front of her house when I left. She smiled as I passed, and in her own inimitable way she said, "God luv ya, Hughie; it's grand to see ya home again."

"Thanks, Lizzie," I replied, "it's good to be home, and it's nice to see you looking so well."

Other neighbors nodded without speaking as I made my way down the street, where leftover rain from the night before made small puddles on the slabbed sidewalk. A group of girls were skipping in the middle of the road. They stopped and looked as I approached, and in a stage whisper I heard one inform the others, "Here's Hughie Gorman; he's outta jail again." As I passed, they all chorused, "Hello, Hughie," then continued skipping and singing their happy little song.

Other boys and girls were playing hopscotch outside Bella Edgar's fish-'n'-chips shops, while two boys swung wildly from yellow straw ropes which they'd tied to the lamp post across the street.

Turning the corner into Donegall Road, I heard someone call my name; and, looking over, I saw my cousin Joe and some other guys. They were standing at the corner of Donegall Road and Innes Place, where up above the door hung a white canvas banner with the words in bold red letters:

Church of the Nazarene
Old-fashioned Gospel Campaign
Evangelist—Rev. Clifford Filer, Wales

I knew the place and remembered it had changed hands so many times. The last time I passed, it was a girls' club; before that it was a practice room for Ross's Flute

Band, in which my father was a member; previous to that it was Coulter's Mission Hall, and now it was the Donegall Road Church of the Nazarene. Boy, I thought, what will that place be next?

The fellows standing there weren't the religious type, so maybe it wasn't too bad. However, I didn't stop, but waved and walked on, for there was something about churches that made me uncomfortable.

At the clock bar, on the corner of Sandy Row, I saw Phil. He was wearing a frayed cloth cap and a heavy overcoat with the collar turned up. A cigarette was dangling from his lips, and his hands were dug deeply into the pockets of the coat. He was standing there, hoping I'd come along and buy him a drink, so we made our way to the notorious Harbor Bar.

Sandy Row is one of the wildest streets in Belfast and known for its drunken brawls and vandalism. If there is any bar worse than the others, it's the Harbor Bar. There you'll find the toughest of "the Row's" hard men, the most provocative of her hookers, and the worst dregs of humanity. Hardly a day went by that there wasn't a fight in the place. There the unsuspecting stranger would be mugged and robbed; and if he resisted, he would find a broken glass or bottle jabbed in his face. Well, decent people just don't frequent that place! But then, everybody knew that Phil and I weren't decent, so we could go in any time.

Ventilation in the bar was nonexistent; consequently a thick pall of tobacco smoke hovered over the heads of the patrons, as if suspended from the ceiling. There was the usual barroom hubbub: glasses clinking, someone trying to sing, the conglomeration of voices in endless chatter, impatient customers shouting for more drinks, and the voice of the tired waiter assuring them, "It's comin' right up!"

As we entered, there was a chorus of greetings from

14

those who knew us. John, the barman, came over and whispered, "There're two guys sitting in the back room; they came in here asking for you fellows. Now, they've never been in here before, and nobody knows who they are, so be careful; they look as if they could con the cross off a donkey's back."

Going into the back room, we found the fellows at a corner table. We knew them from prison. In another corner sat a stranger with a teenage girl who was not of age to be there. They all looked up as we entered. Glaring at the girl, and pointing my thumb at the door, I quietly said, "Scram!"

She pounced out of the chair like a tiger, shouting, "Wha'd'ya mean, Gormey? Who d'ya think y'are?"

"Out, Nan!"

"Ya don't own this place or me."

"You get outta here before I send someone to tell your da."

Nan bestowed one of her powerful Irish blessings (or was it a curse?) before stomping out, followed by her half-drunk, red-faced older companion.

The two ex-cons were wanting to know if Phil and I were interested in getting some easy money. Phil jumped at the opportunity without thinking. I hesitated; but with all my attempts at finding work shattered, I decided to go in with them. We planned a little break-'n'-enter job for the following week.

We sat there drinking until suppertime, when the two fellows had to leave, so Phil and I decided we'd go and have something to eat and meet again at seven. Before leaving the bar, I bought a large bottle of wine and put it in my pocket, then decided to go home by the back streets to avoid the crowds on the main streets. As I turned the corner, I bumped into my cousin who'd been standing at the Church of the Nazarene earlier. Wanting to be friendly, I offered him a drink from the bottle of wine.

"No, thanks, Hughie," he replied, "it's been two years since I've touched that stuff. I'm a Christian now, and since Christ came into my life, it's been transformed. I just don't have any time for liquor, and I'm a happier and a healthier man without it."

I just couldn't believe my ears. He sure sounded different—polite and gentlemanly. And to think he used to be a notorious drinker and brawler. He went on to tell me that all the people in the Nazarene church were praying for me. I thought the guy had flipped his lid, so I got away from that scene as fast as I could.

Thankfully, I managed to get home without bumping into any other street preachers. But in the house I had a temperance lecture from my mother, a scowl of disapproval from my father, and a fish-'n'-chips supper, washed down by a bottle of wine; then I was ready for another good drinking spree.

Before I could get out of the house, my mother cornered me and pleaded with me to stay home. When I refused, she got angry and shouted, "You're like some demented, savage throwback! I don't know in the name of God where you came from, or what crime it was I committed to be harnessed with you, or where it is your drinking's going to land you, for you're getting worse . . ."

Pushing her to the side, I left the house uttering a volley of profanity, to the accompaniment of bitter sobbing.

Back in the bar, I learned there was a change in plans, and I had to meet Phil in the Loyola Bar in Sandy Row. I found him in one of the side rooms in the company of a man of means, who apparently was a big spender and who was already higher than a kite. It looked like we were in for a good night on the town, as we made merry, drinking and singing. But all too soon the waiter came in shouting, "Time, gentlemen, please! Last orders, please!" After gulping down one more drink, we left the bar to make our way to a social club in May Street, where we could drink all night to our hearts' content (or so we thought).

Stepping out into the night, I saw a crowd and thought there was a brawl, until I heard someone singing:

> *So I'll cherish the old rugged Cross,*
> *Till my trophies at last I lay down.*
> *I will cling to the old rugged Cross,*
> *And exchange it someday for a crown.*

Stopping to listen, I recognized the singer as Stewart Atkinson, a notorious drunkard, who sang in all the bars in Sandy Row for free drinks and was hardly ever sober. There he was, looking so well, singing for the good-livin' people, and sober as a judge. I also recognized some of his cronies, including my cousin. I turned to walk away before any of them approached me; but just as I turned, a man in a clerical collar stepped in front of me, took hold of my arm as he looked me in the eye, and said, "Gorman, God can change your life." I just shook him off and laughed as I walked after my friends.

On our way to the club we saw a lot of that unique side of Belfast's Saturday night—the activity on the city streets as the evangelical Christians go into action. There's no place quite like it. After getting away from the Nazarene street meeting, we'd only gone three blocks when we passed the people from Sandy Row Methodist Church, who were also conducting a street meeting. Cutting through Hope Street to Great Victoria Street, we were confronted by the Baptists, who presented us with gospel tracts and invited us to church. Next we passed a "stupid old fool" wearing sandwich boards, the front of which read "We Are Fools for Christ's Sake," and on the back the question, "Whose Fool Are You?" Before getting to the club, we heard the Plymouth Brethren sounding forth somewhere in the direction of Donegall Square.

The three of us sat drinking and singing in the club until about 2:30 in the morning, when the barman refused to serve us any more. "You've had enough and are making too much noise," he informed us; "I think you'd better go." With that we were escorted to the door by a huge, flat-nosed, heavyweight bouncer, who looked as tall and as broad as the side of a house. None of us were prepared to remonstrate with him.

Outside, Phil and I decided it was time to bid farewell to our wealthy benefactor and relieve him of any possessions he had. I pushed him against the wall; and as I did so, a large wine bottle smashed down on his balding head, leaving slivers of glass embedded in his flesh, which glistened in the light of the street lamp. Tiny beads of blood formed at the base of each sliver of glass. Startled, I let go of him, and he ran down May Street in the direction of the markets, but we had no trouble catching him. Falling to the ground, he tried to protect himself from the blows raining down upon him, and I heard his desperate prayer, "O dear Jesus, please don't let them kill me." He was still mumbling prayers as we emptied his wallet and pockets, and took his watch and ring, before giving him a few extra kicks to let him know how stupid we thought he was.

The shrill, piercing blast of a police whistle shattered the night air and paralyzed us for a moment. It was enough to wake the dead in Dublin. To the man on the ground it was an answer to prayer. To Phil and me it was like the sound of a starter's pistol, and as there was no time to get ready or set, we just had to go. And go we did! We ran neck 'n' neck in the direction of the markets, until I cut 'round by the telephone exchange and into Joy Street, where I ran into the open door of a terrace house. The house was in darkness; but I stood behind the door for a long time before slowly emerging and walking to Sandy Row, where I established an alibi before going home.

I can't remember all that happened that week, especially at night. Sometimes I'd walk home . . . or ride a taxi . . . or be carried, but there were nights when I didn't know what I'd been doing. During those days I lived in fear that I'd do something really dreadful while in an alcoholic stupor, but it wasn't enough to keep me from the bar.

Saturday night rolled around again, and I was drinking in the Loyola Bar. At closing time I came out to be confronted again by the Nazarenes who were having their weekly street meeting. About 15 people stood around in a circle, singing gospel songs; from time to time one would step out into the centre of the circle to sing or shout or testify.

I knew there was something different about those people; they certainly weren't like the bunch I'd associated with all my life. I'd only been standing there a minute or two when Bert Kelly had me by the arm, looked me straight in the eye, and challenged me with those same words, "Gorman, God can change your life."

I just laughed, but he held on to me this time and continued, "Listen, we're having special services at the church. There's a great preacher there from Wales; I'm sure you'd be interested in what he has to say. Will you come?"

"Sure," I lied, "I'll be there!"

"That's great," exclaimed Mr. Kelly. "I'll send someone to call for you at a quarter to seven tomorrow evening."

I laughed as I walked away, though not through disrespect, for I liked these people and knew that they were out to help others. I laughed at what the man said: "God can change your life!" The poor guy actually thought that there was some great, supernatural God who could change people's lives. I didn't believe that!

It wasn't that I didn't want my life changed, for there wasn't a man in all of Ireland who wanted to be changed as much as I. In fact there wasn't a person who hated himself as much as I hated Hugh Gorman—the person I was, the things I did, my own weakness. Deep down in my heart I wanted to be different; but it just wasn't possible.

"God can change your life!" Those words mocked me! But if only it were true, how glad I'd be. But why even think about it? Other people had tried to change my life—my own parents—and failed; they failed miserably! And if they couldn't change my life, what could God do?

2

Red Brick Jungle

Sandy Row, where they keep no Sunday;
And every day's like an Easter Monday.

That's how the lyricist immortalized the area of Belfast where I was born and raised. Sandy Row is known to almost every Irishman; and people from near and far have seen pictures of the district and its residents on television. "The Row," as it's affectionately called, is one of the notorious extremist Protestant districts in Belfast. It's a typical working-class area of stringy street after street of small, flat-faced, red-brick terraced houses. The red is blackened by years of industrial pollution, and messed further by the obscene sectarian graffiti. It's a red brick jungle!

Devoid of lawns or gardens, there's not a blade of grass to be seen. Each house is small, without shape, but built to last. Comfort plays but a small part in the overall design of the house, whose front door is right on the sidewalk. A front hall, with a room off it, leads to a kitchen-cum-scullery in which there are two other doors; one leads to a bedroom or dining room, and the other to a tiny backyard.

The yard is closed in, with just enough space for a garbage bin, a bag of coal, a clothesline. The most modern thing is the toilet, which is against the back wall in a red-brick cubicle. There's no fleecy soft toilet tissue in the cubicle; a small box nailed to the wall contains cut-up squares of the *Belfast Telegraph*.

Upstairs, each house has two tiny bedrooms and a small landing. There's no bathroom, and bathing is done in the kitchen sink. Needless to say, many of these houses have been reduced to uninhabitable slums by vandalism and sectarian violence.

This ghetto has been a hotbed of extremism and an ideal recruiting ground for young terrorist gunmen and assassins. The people are fanatically proud of the fact that they are all Protestants, and sing with great zeal:

Up Sandy Row, where the Fenians [Catholics] never go,
On the twelfth of July in the morning.

Into this area came Rev. William (Bert) Kelly, a dedicated minister of the gospel. His task? To raise up a center for holiness evangelism—the Church of the Nazarene. His district superintendent, Dr. George Frame, had given him no mean assignment, for Sandy Row was a modern jungle, where young people learned early how to gamble, to drink, to steal, to fight, and, of course, to hate Catholics.

Bert Kelly was a Belfastman and knew Sandy Row, having worked there previously as a city missionary. But I knew the district better than Bert would ever know it, for it was there I was born and lived for the first 22 years of my life. This story really starts about the time Pastor Kelly was getting things moving in his new home mission Church of the Nazarene.

Eureka Street, in West Belfast's Sandy Row area, is one of the thousands of streets built under the shadows of Ireland's giant linen mills. Entering the street from the east, there is an excellent view of the beautiful Divis

Mountains. The street, running parallel with Donegall Road, is about 200 yards long and is almost filled, side by side, with tiny red-brick terrace houses. There are 65 houses in the street, 40 on the north side and 25 on the south, all crammed in between: St. Aidan's church hall on the northeast corner; Bella Edgars fish-'n'-chips shop on the southeast corner; Felt Street Mission Hall on the northwest corner; and the great, hospitallike Cripples Institute, which filled the southwest side of the street. Under the shadow of this building sat Harry Armstrong's stable yard, with its two horses, three wagons, two wirehaired fox terriers, a multitude of rats, a good supply of coal briquettes, and lots of fruit and vegetables.

The people of Eureka Street are loyal to the British Crown and ever so proud of the exploits of King William III, even though the same gentleman has been dead and gone for more than 200 years. Every July, the people celebrate King Billy's victory over King James and his Catholic forces at the historic battle at the river Boyne in 1690. Every house proudly displays its British and/or Ulster flag. A gigantic, brilliantly illuminated archway is built across the street, on which is painted the names of places where the Protestant forces fought with distinction; Londonderry, Aughrim, Enniskillen, the river Boyne.

On the arch, large amplifiers blare out militant Protestant music day and night. Into the early hours of the morning there'll be singing and dancing in the streets; and then on the night of the 11th of July, at eleven o'clock, a huge bonfire is lit at the east end of the street, and people of all ages sing and dance around the fire until it goes out.

The 12th of July is the big day when the celebrations reach their climax. This is the day when the Orange Order puts on its colossal display of strength. Orangemen dressed in their Sunday best, many wearing bowler hats, carrying rolled umbrellas, and silver swords or ancient pikes, and all of them wearing their orange or blue sashes, will join their lodges for the annual parade to Finaghy.

The women and children don't join the parade, but do gather in their thousands along the parade route, to wave their flags, cheer their men, and sing their Ulster loyalist songs:

> *Sure it's old, but it is beautiful,*
> *And its colors they are fine;*
> *It was worn at Derry, Aughrim,*
> *Enniskillen, and the Boyne.*
> *Sure my father wore it, when in youth,*
> *In bygone days of yore;*
> *And it's on the twelfth I love to wear*
> *The sash my father wore.*

Up to 50,000 men will march in the parade, behind beautiful colored banners on which have been painted some of the great heroes of the faith: Luther, Calvin, Wesley, Knox, and others. What a variety of bands there are in the parade: pipe, flute, brass, silver, accordion, and string. There are bands from all parts of Ireland, some from Scotland, and even as far away as Toronto, Canada; and each one is greeted with enthusiastic applause. The parade is watched by hundreds of thousands along the route, and by millions on television.

In the evening the men come home tired and weary, and with their wives sit down to watch the replay of the parade on the rented black-and-white television. Children gather in the streets to have their own mini-parade, with tin drums, pot lids, plastic whistles, and paper flags. For hours they'll march up and down the street, led by a tiny drum major, who has commandeered his mother's broom. At the top of their voices they'll sing the songs they heard their father sing:

> *We'll fight and "No Surrender!"*
> *We'll guard old Derry's walls;*

24

With heart, and hand, and sword, and shield,
We'll guard old Derry's walls.

None of the people in Eureka Street own their own houses. They're all rented from the "landlord," Mr. Robinson, who every Friday goes from door to door, collecting the weekly rent of 10 shillings and 6 pence. No one envies him his job, for he sure doesn't have an easy time collecting his money. Many of the people are reluctant to pay; there are some who won't pay, and others who cannot pay. Often the rentman will be met at the door by a barefooted, ragged, and dirty little boy or girl who will inform him, "Me ma says she's not in, Mr. Robinson."

There's lots of fun in the street. If the residents don't provide their own entertainment, there'll be visitors who'll come along and do it for them. There's sweet Gypsy Rose, who'll tell your fortune, pray for you, or slit your throat for a "silver shilling." Ginger, the ragged male troubador, will sing and dance from one end of the street to the other for pennies. Old Paddy, the ragman, is happy to give you a cup 'n' saucer, a toy balloon, or a goldfish in a water-filled plastic bag, in exchange for your big bundle of old rags. Larry, the big, fat, chain-smoking bin man, will carry your garbage from the backyard, through the scullery and living room, to the street, where it will sit for hours while children search through the smelly trash until the truck comes. Big Sammy will come knocking from door to door, asking for "old refuse," with which he feeds his prime Irish porkers. Then there is the milkman, coal man, fish man, gas meter man, electric meter man, television rental man, insurance man, the inevitable drunk, and at least a dozen debt collectors. All of these have their own peculiar characteristics and make their contribution to a variety in the life of the street.

One man I didn't mention— the ever unpopular school attendance inspector, who for some unknown reason was called "the school board," although that wasn't the worst name he was called. He made his appearance in the street to the accompaniment of boos and jeers from all the children. His responsibility was to inform the parents when, and how often, their children were absent from school. The parents didn't always know when their children were absent, so Mr. Brown was often the bearer of bad tidings.

In Sandy Row, being absent from school without parents' permission was a very common happening. I know, for I used to enjoy it. In Belfast it was called "mitching," and I was the undisputed mitcher in our house; hardly a week went by that I wasn't absent at least one day.

On one occasion I stayed away from school for two weeks before my mother found out. My father was away at sea at the time. Each morning I'd leave the house when it was time to go to school, hide my schoolbag, and then make my way to the docks, the horse fair, the coal brick yard, the tramcar depot, or the market. I'd just wander from place to place, enjoying the freedom away from home and school. Always I'd arrive home in time for supper, thinking I was a pretty smart fellow! But . . .

One day on entering the house, I came face-to-face with old Mr. Brown, the school board. "Where have you been for the past two weeks, Hugh?" he wanted to know.

"At school," I answered him, while looking at my mother.

"You know right well you haven't been at school," thundered Mr. Brown.

"Well, I'm not going back to school."

"And why not?"

"Because I don't like it; it's a waste of time."

"If you refuse to go to school, we'll put you in Malone Training School."

"I won't go there either."

"You'll have no say in the matter."

"And why not?"

"Because you'll be taken there by the police."

"You can't make me stay there."

"Oh, yes, we can; and you'll be locked in day and night."

"Yeah, that's what you think; they'll have to catch me first."

"Mr. Brown," my mother interjected, "please leave Hugh to me, and I'll make sure he's in school tomorrow morning."

"Mrs. Gorman," he replied, "if he isn't in school tomorrow, you'll be in court to explain to the magistrate. It could be that the court will find he's in need of care and protection, and you could lose your boy."

Having received my mother's assurance, Mr. Brown left me to explain where I'd been going for the past two weeks, and why. My explanation didn't satisfy an angry mother, who gave me a severe walloping.

All the kids in Eureka Street attended the same schools in Blythe Street, which was only two blocks away. At the age of five they started in junior public elementary school, and went through junior and senior infants, and classes one to three. Then they passed to the senior public elementary school, where there were classes four to seven. All of the students finished school when they reached the age of 14 whether they got to grade seven or not. Although most of the kids did reach the top grade, they were never encouraged to continue their education. We lived on the wrong side of the tracks and were needed to work in the cheap-labor linen mills and factories, to multiply the wealth of the lords of Ireland. In saunalike conditions, boys and girls would sweat it out for nine hours each day for a pittance.

Even though parents in our street were proud of their

great Protestant heritage, they never attended church, not even at Easter or Christmas. Some of the women attended the meetings in the mission halls which abounded in the area. But religiously they sent their children to Sunday school every Sunday; and there was no shortage of Sunday schools in the district, for there was at least one in every street.

I don't know if my parents were more religious than the others, or just glad to be rid of us for two hours every Sunday, but they sent us to Sunday school twice every week. In the morning we would go to Matilda Street Gospel Hall, and in the afternoon to Felt Street Mission Hall. I've the feeling we went mostly for the loaves and fishes. Mothers knew if they sent their children to certain Sunday schools they'd be rewarded by free coal tickets, food parcels, blankets, clothes, and the annual mammoth Christmas hamper. They also knew when there were free dinners and free summer camps, and took full advantage of it.

I lived longer in 53 Eureka Street than any other place. It was a typical Ulster Protestant home. On the wall, above the fireplace, hung a beautiful picture of Queen Elizabeth II; on another wall was a large picture of King William III on his gallant white charger, as he crossed the river Boyne in pursuit of King James and his merry men. Then there were framed certificates from the Loyal Orange Lodge and the Royal Black Institute, belonging to my father. Newspapers, magazines, and political propaganda, lying around, indicated that we were in favor of Northern Ireland's union with Great Britain, and opposed to the Irish Republican Army's ambition of a united Ireland under a Roman Catholic government in Dublin.

When all our family got together in our little house, we were like sardines in a can, for it was chock-a-block full. Besides my parents, there was Davie, myself, Tommy,

Anne, Jimmy, and Josey. There had been two other children, Jackie and Margaret, who died in infancy. Upstairs there were two bedrooms, but we didn't always have two beds, for I remember when we only had one double bed and one crib. And the crib, which held two, was always in use. There were times when four of us had to sleep in the bed—two at the head and two at the foot. We didn't mind— it was nice and cosy; and we thought it was quite normal, for most of the people in the street did the same.

And we were just like the other people, poor and overcrowded, with drinking problems, gambling problems, and the usual family fights on Friday or Saturday night. But Mother would always try to keep us from getting into trouble, and she worried when we were out of her sight. As soon as we'd come in, she'd ask us, "Where've you been? Who were you with? What were you doing?" And, of course, back in those days mothers weren't always told the truth, nor even half the truth.

Our street was full of petty crooks. My mother used to declare, "They'd steal the eye outta your head and come back for your eyelashes." I wasn't very old when I joined the ranks of the petty criminals and started stealing at home, first from my mother's purse, often taking all she had, then from my father's wallet. When Dad came home on Friday and Saturday night, he was often so drunk he didn't know how much money he had; so I used to help myself and he never missed it.

I was 12 when I started working for Harry Armstrong and his son, Bobby. They owned the stable yard and store across the street from us and sold fruit, vegetables, fish, coal briquettes, and coke (for fires).

One day in the stable yard, I was cleaning up when my friend Herbie dropped in to see me, and we had some fun horsing around. Being in a mischievous mood, I threw a rotten apple at him, hitting him right between the eyes. To me it was a great joke; but not to Herbie, who was so enraged that he lifted a knife and threw it. It hit me across the back of my wrist, cutting to the bone, and sending blood spurting all over the place.

Herbie took off fast to his house across the street, slamming the door behind him. Picking up the knife, I took after him, thumping and kicking the door, and calling him all sorts of filthy names. But there was no way he was going to open the door, knowing I was mad and in possession of the knife. Some of the neighbors got hold of me and took me to the hospital, where several stitches were put in the wound. Because of it I wasn't able to go to school for two weeks, by which time Herbie and I were the best of friends again.

It was a great day when, at the age of 14, I started working in the Blackstaff Spinning and Weaving Company on the Springfield Road. For the first time in my life I was thrown right into the midst of a mass of Roman Catholics. To my great surprise I found that they were very ordinary people, just like myself(?). None of them tried to poison me, cut my throat, stick a knife in my back, drop a bale on me, or throw me down an elevator shaft, as I'd been told they might do. I enjoyed being with them more than being at work, and I still remember with joy some of my first Roman Catholic friends.

Work in the mill lasted just over a year before I was *fired.* My job was to oil all the textile machinery, and I was warned time and time again that the fibre was highly flammable, so it was dangerous to smoke. But I just had to have a cigarette! And I had a good opportunity to do it, for I started work an hour before all the others and began the day with a smoke. One morning I was doing just that– sitting beside a bag of flax–and decided to see if the stuff really *was* highly flammable.

Picking up a piece of flax, I put a match to it;

immediately it blazed up and burned my fingers, causing me to drop it—right into the bag of flax, which went up in flames, and caught the fibre on the nearby machines. For a while it seemed as if the whole room were on fire, and I had visions of the whole mill going up in smoke; but I managed to get the fire out, yet not before there was considerable damage. Before I had time to think about what had happened, I was a former employee of the Blackstaff— *fired!*

After this incident I didn't work for a long time but loitered around, getting into all kinds of mischief; consequently I was in one hassle after another with my parents. I decided to run away from home, and planned going to Dublin, which is 100 miles away. Not having enough money to take me all the way, I bought a one-way ticket to Portadown, from where I could hitch a ride to my destination. Good thinking, but . . .

It was a cold and windy night when I arrived in Portadown and headed south for Dublin. I crossed the bridge and walked out of town into the dark Ulster countryside, where there were no lamps, only thorny hedges, stone walls, and earthen banks bound by grass. I walked steadily for a long time without seeing another person. Once I heard footsteps and slowed down a little. A tall man came out of the dark, crossed to the other side of the road, and passed me. He didn't speak, and neither did I. I stopped for a while to listen to the retreating footsteps and didn't hear them. I moved, and stopped, and heard them— running! We were each afraid of what we were going to meet in the dark. The passing stranger's fears intensified my own, and I walked faster.

With about 10 good Irish miles behind me, the road seemed to get darker, and I began to imagine all sorts of things. What was it I heard? The wind was howling through the trees, making a variety of unearthly noises, but there was something else. I was convinced that there were all sorts of ghosts, banshees, and evil Irish spirits abroad that night. Oh, yes, I was scared, and would rather have faced my parents with all their nagging than be alone with the unknown in the dark, eerie countryside of County Armagh.

Fear and indecision brought me to a halt; and in the dark it didn't matter if I went north or south, they both looked the same. If only a car would come! I hadn't seen a vehicle for hours, and I was getting colder and on the border of panic. If I ever get home, I told myself, I'll *never* leave it again! Then I saw the lights; it was a van going north, and I put my thumb out, praying, "Oh, mister, please stop!" He did!

"Where on earth are you going at this hour of the night, man?"

"To Belfast, mister."

"Aye, you sure sound as if you come from the Shankill Road, do you?"

"No, mister, I'm from the Donegall Road," I lied, afraid to tell him I was from a Protestant district in case he was a wild IRA terrorist.

"Well, jump in," he said, "I'll take you as far as Lurgan; that's as far as I'm going."

I was never as glad for a ride in all my life, even though it was only to Lurgan. There I went to the police barracks to see if they'd let me stay until morning. They wouldn't even open the door but peeped through an observation hole and told me to be on my way, as they weren't running a hotel. They gave me an address of what they called a "cheap lodging house," and I went there.

I knocked on the door and the house with the sign "Bed and Breakfast," and it seemed ages before anyone came to answer.

"Who's there?" asked a woman from within.

"I'm looking for a bed for the night, missus," I told her.

I could hear the bolt being drawn, and the door opened slowly. A middle-aged woman stood there in her nightie.

"I've one bed left," she informed me. "I hope you don't mind sleeping in the same room with three other men?"

"That's all right."

"It's nothing fancy."

"It'll do just fine, missus."

"Come on in; it'll be three shillings in advance."

After a night spent tossing, turning, and scratching, I took to the road again and thumbed a ride to Belfast. As soon as I crossed the threshold at home, I was right into the battle again with my parents. There was just no way I could avoid it. Even so, I was glad to be home again, rather than on that dark Dublin road. But being home didn't solve my problems.

I can remember the many times my mother stood weeping, pleading with me to come out of a house of ill repute, or to come out of a bar, and give up drinking and carousing. How often I cursed and slammed the door in her face, knowing I was breaking her heart; but I couldn't care less.

My parents were determined to keep after me until I changed my ways, and they put a lot of effort into it. But they failed! They couldn't change my life! Yet, the preacher from the Nazarene church, Bert Kelly, stood in Sandy Row, telling me, "Gorman, God can change your life."

How could He? My parents, who were responsible for bringing me into the world and raising me, had tried and couldn't. Why, even the almost almighty British Army had tried some of their "never fail" methods to change me. After more than four years, they gave up in exasperation. How did this pastor think that his great God, who was away up in heaven, could do what people on earth had failed to do?

3

Caribbean Capers

You'll see 'em wherever you are: in Soho, in Timbuctoo, even in Kansas City. Irishmen, I mean! For centuries, Erin has sent millions of her sons and daughters to the uttermost parts of the earth, blown by the four winds on the seven seas. Born with restless spirits, disillusioned by bigotry in their motherland, they've never been able to resist the lure of those exciting, faraway places.

I've heard those happy wanderers reminisce about the Khyber Pass, Singapore, Kuala Lumpur, the Zambezi, and many other places with exotic names. From childhood I've dreamt of travelling to the tropics, meeting different people, and enjoying the whole world. Yes, I longed for that day when I could go to Montego Bay, Famagusta, or even Port Said–any place to get away from home.

My day came when I was 17. After some conflict and lots of pleading, my parents finally said I could join the army. The picture in the window read, "For Excitement and Adventure–Join an Irish Regiment in the British Army."

That's just what I wanted to do and walked boldly into the office.

"Can I help you?" asked a tall Irish guardsman from behind the counter. In double quick time I'd filled in all the forms, had a medical examination, taken the oath of allegiance to the British Crown, and received a token day's pay of seven shillings, and then the recruiting officer proudly informed me, "Gorman, you're in the army now!"

It was cold and wet when we arrived at the training depot of the North Irish Brigade in County Down. The new recruits were shown into a khaki army Nissen hut which had no heating; but the corporal told us not to worry, as he would make sure we each had two blankets. And he was true to his word! We each received two regulation "army blankets, grey," and every one of us shivered all through the night.

Next morning we were paraded to the quartermaster's store, where we received our uniforms and equipment. When this was all neatly packed away in our bedside locker, army life started in earnest. That nice corporal seemed to have changed overnight, for he was no longer the friendly individual who'd welcomed us the night before.

"Everyone pay attention," he bellowed. "In five minutes, I want every one of you properly dressed, in denims, boots, gaiters, berets, and on the parade ground! Any questions?"

"Yes, mister—" someone began but got no further.

"What's your name, soldier?" demanded the corporal, as he walked up to the soldier.

"It's Mike Clancey, mister, but—"

"Soldier, when I ask who you are, I want you to give me your regimental number, your rank, and your surname. Got that?"

"Yes, mi—"

"Now, who are you?"

"22–26–46–41, Fusilier Clancey, mister."

"Now, one more thing I want you to remember, and this goes for all of you. You see these two stripes on my arm? They're to let you know that I'm a corporal. When you address me, you address me as 'corporal.' I'm not 'mister' to anybody! And when you speak to me, or I speak to you, you stand up straight, heels together, tummy in, chest out, head back, and hands by your side, with your thumbs by the seam in your pants. You got that, soldier?"

"Yes, mis—corporal."

"Good! Now, make sure you don't forget it; for if you do, I'll have you in the guardroom so fast your feet won't touch the ground."

And that was only the beginning! There was more to come—much more! On the parade ground we were to have our first meeting with the platoon sergeant. He was a Goliath of a man, with hands like forklifts and a voice like sandpaper. Smartly dressed in regimental uniform with red sash, and carrying a pacing stick, he was every inch a soldier. He looked us over, from left to right, head to toe, and back to front, with a sneer of disgust on his face.

"So you want to be soldiers?" He laughed sarcastically. "Well, that's what I'm here for—to make rough, tough, fighting, disciplined soldiers—professional killers! But look at the state of you! I can tell you now, some of you aren't gonna make it. Before this week is out—yeah, before this day is over—some of you'll be on sick parade, trying to get into the hospital, trying to get a medical discharge. Others are gonna run away over the border into the Irish Republic, where you came from. Every last one of you'll curse me, wish me dead; or you'll wish that you were dead. But get this into your thick skulls—I'm gonna make soldiers of you, or I'll take extreme pleasure in breaking you in the process . . ."

After listening to that battle-crazed old war-horse, and a
few others like him, I thought of the words

> *I don't want no more of army life,*
>> *Oh, Ma, I wanna go . . .*
>> *Hey, Ma, I wanna go home.*

That's how I felt at the end of the day. I was sick of
regimental maniacs telling me what to do, how to do it,
when to do it, and what would happen to me if I didn't do it.
I knew there and then that I was in the wrong outfit, and
army life just wasn't for me, and I vowed I wouldn't stay
one day longer than necessary. From that point I went to
work to get out as quickly and as quietly as possible.

I am amazed at how easy it was for me to get into the
army, but was alarmed at how difficult it was to get out. I
didn't serve my five years in the regular army, as my
discharge book reveals that I served for four years and 103
days. The major part of that was spent undergoing punishment for a variety of offences. In my attempt to get out of
the army, I crossed swords with the establishment many
times and was charged with and punished for: being
drunk, insubordination, dumb insolence (just a smile at the
wrong time), common assault, wilful defiance of an order,
absence from parade, armed assault whilst on active
service, forcing a safeguard to lay down his arms, absent
without leave, etc.

My royal initials— H. H. G.— are scratched on the walls of
military prison cells in Jamaica, Belize, Ireland, England,
Cyprus, Egypt, and in the brig on board troopships on
which I travelled.

Now, even though I didn't like being in the army, I did
my best to make life as interesting as possible. And there
weren't too many dull moments, especially when we were
on the move to different parts of the world.

Travelling was what thrilled me more than anything. It
was great meeting people in different parts of the world,

observing their customs, and having travel experiences which were only dreams in the past. We were excited when we learned that our regiment was to have a tour of duty in the Caribbean area. What a trip that was! Ballykinlar Camp to Belize, via Belfast, Liverpool, and the Azores—the first of those mysterious places with the strange-sounding names.

The visit to the Azores intensified the excitement and anticipation of the men, who just longed to see more of these beautiful islands and meet more of these beautiful people from other lands. Our next port of call was Hamilton, in the island of Bermuda. What a gorgeous island that is, with its multiplicity of colored flowers. It was easy to see that Bermuda was a popular tourist paradise, especially for the rich American, Canadian, and British, but not for the poor British soldier. We enjoyed our visit but longed to be on our way again.

"Fascinated" is the only word to describe our reactions as we watched the many creatures of the sea as we stood by the rail of the ship in mid-Atlantic. Dolphins swam around the ship at amazing speed; flying fish put on a display for our benefit, some even landing on the deck for our amusement; and from time to time sharks would surface, making us glad that we were on board ship and not in the briny deep.

Not only were we to see how beautiful the Atlantic can be, but that great ocean put on a spectacular performance, revealing how awful she can be when she desires. The captain announced we were approaching a storm area. We had an unscheduled, but expected, lifeboat drill–and then it came! I never dreamed that it was possible for the sea to be so ferocious. That giant of a ship seemed to be uncontrollable, as it was tossed from wave to wave, like a huge football, at the mercy of an angry sea. At one point, the ship made an unbelievable 180-degree turn around, and those who were battling seasickness were terror stricken. Big, tough soldiers and veteran sailors crowded the washrooms. Some couldn't make it and just lay on their hammocks, or on the deck, helpless.

We were later told that the ship had run into the tail end of a hurricane that wasn't supposed to have come our way. What d'ya think about that? One of those big-shot army officers slipped up and failed to inform the tail of the hurricane. But there was no turning back, so southwestward—ho!

As we sailed by the Bahamas, and through the strait between Cuba and Haiti, all was so inspiring and serene. Next day, we were told, we'd be in Kingston, Jamaica, where an advance party would disembark and prepare the camp for those who would be stationed there. One day's shore leave was granted to all the men, and after the storm, which had generated so much fear and tension, everybody was looking forward to being on terra firma again.

None of the islanders could remember an Irish regiment being stationed in Jamaica, and they were wondering what kind of people we were. Our regiment was taking over from an English regiment which was still on the island. It was a day to be remembered—by the native population, by the bar owners, and the civil and military police.

I can't remember how, when, or where it happened, but I was one of the many arrested for being drunk and disorderly, and taken to the detention cells. All I remember is being awakened in a cell and being transported to the ship, where I was bawled out by an irate company sergeant major, before being placed in another cell to await trial. As the ship headed out to sea, destined for Belize, I was marched before my company commander, who sentenced me to "seven days confined to barracks."

The harbor at Belize is too shallow for large, oceangoing liners; so our ship docked about a mile from shore, where we boarded huge barges and were towed to shore. The 100 men of A company proceeded to their new quarters at Airport Camp, some miles from the city. We were all delighted to be away from the remainder of the regiment, and especially from the regimental sergeant major, and the provost sergeant, the two official bullies of the regiment.

Belize, for me, was one big nine-month drinking spree, for during that time all I lived for was rum, women, and song. But the cheap white Honduran rum was getting to me as no other liquor had. From the first week I was in Belize, when I fought with a cab driver and smashed all the windows in his cab, until the time I left, I was continually in trouble with the civil and military authorities. Because of my heavy drinking and the kind of living that accompanied it, the time came when I could no longer carry out my military duties. So, my company commander, being fed up with me, shipped me back to headquarters in Jamaica, where I was in hospital for three weeks before I was able to resume some military responsibilities.

Because of violent confrontations with the Jamaicans, not many of the soldiers would venture to downtown Kingston, but stayed close to camp. Things got worse when one of the officers shot and killed a young Jamaican, who was attempting to break into the officers' quarters. Poor old Alf, the officer, in defending himself, is reputed to have said, "I didn't know the gun was loaded"; so the song with that title was sung enthusiastically in the canteen for many nights.

One night some of the lads were evicted from the Cross Roads Club; and others were refused entry, which caused a scene at the door. The news of this spread, and soon there were scores of Irish soldiers gathered outside, just itching for a fight. It happened so quickly! Without any leadership,

40

the mob stampeded right into the club, beating up the employees, molesting the customers, and wrecking the furnishings. On their way out they stole everything they could get their hands on. What a night!

Before leaving the island, I had one more confrontation with the mighty military powers. It happened one night when I was confined to barracks for being absent from parade. I was bored stiff, craving for a drink, but had no money. Packing a bag full of my buddies' gear, I skipped out of camp to the nearest honky-tonk bar, which was out of bounds to military personnel. There I auctioned off the gear, item by item, to raise drinking money. The sale was going pretty good, and I was having a great time, until a patrol of regimental police came in and caught me in the act. That night I was in familiar surroundings—the old guardroom cell, where I scraped another x beside my name on the wall.

Taken before my commanding officer, I was given this advice: "Gorman, you've just about completed half your five years. It has been two and a half hectic years, for you just jump in and out of trouble more than any person I know. Why don't you change your way of going, turn over a new leaf, and start soldiering the way a man ought to in this regiment? I will give you all the help I can, but you must do your part. I know you can do it; will you try?"

I promised I would try, and did try, but alas! I wasn't successful. I was weak in the face of peer pressure; and before long I gave in to my buddies and surrendered to the bar and the bottle. There was just no way of changing me at that time. Yet, at the back of my mind, I was thinking that when I got back to Britain, it would be different, but not just then.

4

Egyptian Escapades

One of the most beautiful sights for those returning from overseas to Britain is the majestic white cliffs of Dover. On top of those cliffs sits the stately Dover Castle, like a picture from medieval history. I was stationed in the castle on my return from Jamaica.

The detention cells in the castle are in an old dungeon, where passages lead to caves under the cliffs. Here some of the people of Dover sheltered during the German bombardment in World War II. I've walked along those passages and explored the caves, thankful that there were no enemy rockets exploding overhead. The only explosions during my time were the regimental sergeant major and the provost sergeant, who were furious with my attitude and actions.

After being in Dover for a couple of days, I was granted

six weeks' leave and went home to Belfast. The whole thing was a huge nightmare, consisting of drunken brawls, eviction from bars and clubs for causing trouble, and quarrels at home. Finally, my sister was taken to hospital with a gash under her chin, where I kicked her in a drunken rage. She still carries the scar to remind her of that ugly incident.

While I was on leave in Belfast, trouble broke out in the Suez Canal Zone of Egypt. All army leave was cancelled, and servicemen were ordered to return to their units. I'd no difficulty in deciding not to return, but sat in my favorite bar, having a good time with my friends. As we sat there, my father walked in, carrying my bag.

It was obvious that he was extremely annoyed. "Come on," he ordered, "you're going to the boat, or you'd better find another place to live."

After a little bit of unfriendly discussion and finishing my drink, I decided to go. On our way to Donegall Quay, we met one of my army buddies, Skajer, who was also on his way to the boat. At the dockside, my dad was so disgusted with me and so glad to see my back as I walked up the gangway, he didn't even wait to wave good-bye.

The ship was packed with servicemen returning to their units, and most of them seemed to be quite happy about going overseas to "have a go" at the Arabs. Skajer and I had second thoughts on the matter and decided we'd stay in Belfast for another few days. Leaving our bags on the deck, we walked to the gangway, to find it guarded by the military police. After looking for an alternate exit and finding none, we decided to go over the side—no, not into the water, but onto the dockside, where hundreds of friends were seeing the soldiers off. The ship was just casting off when I shouted to Skajer, "Let's go! Jump!"

We both jumped together and landed on our feet. Seeing our comrades sailing down the Belfast Lough on board ship, we thought we'd sing them one of our famous regimental songs of farewell, and together began to sing,

Fare thee well, Inniskillings,
Fare thee well, for a while . . .

We were still singing and waving when a squad of tough military policemen came, literally picked us up, and threw us into the back of the paddy wagon. Our protests and struggles were to no avail, and they drove us across town to Victoria Military Barracks.

Arriving at the barracks, we were taken into the guard-room, where they were preparing for the changing of the guard. Apparently the guards were preoccupied, making sure they were properly dressed. Anyhow, they were unprepared for our arrival, for their loaded weapons were lying on one of the beds. Skajer grabbed a loaded Sten gun and rifle; throwing the rifle to me, he shouted,

"Come on, Hughie, let's get outta here!"

Armed with their weapons, we lined the guards against the wall, backed out of the guardroom, and made our escape. Well, that's what we thought! By the time we got to the camp gates, there was a platoon of armed soldiers waiting for us. They were under the command of the duty officer, who was brandishing a service revolver. And like you see in the movies, he fired a shot over our heads and ordered us to drop our weapons. Being outnumbered, and not wanting to have a shoot-out at the "Bar X," we surrendered to the silly little officer, but not before telling him what we thought of him and his merry men.

The following night we stood again at the Donegall Quay. This time we were handcuffed to two nice military policemen, who assured us they'd make sure we'd be well taken care of until we arrived safely in Dover Castle. And they did! We weren't surprised to find that there was an empty cell reserved for us in the dungeon.

Although what we'd done in Belfast was a court-martial offence, the regimental adjutant eventually freed us. He was up to his neck in work, preparing for our move to the Middle East, and didn't want to be bothered by prisoners or courts-martial. "Listen, you two idiots," he said, "I'm going to release you on open arrest until I hear from the military police in Belfast. For goodness' sake keep out of trouble." We assured him we would, but . . .

We were to leave the castle late at night on the day before sailing to the Mediterranean. The bar and canteen were closed all day, to ensure there'd be no drunks on parade. But where there's a will, there's a way; and we found a way to get all the drink we wanted for our final spree in Dover.

Up to that point we didn't know our exact destination. We simply knew we were to make ourselves available for active service in the Canal Zone of Egypt. What an unexpected joy it was, a few days later, to sail in to Famagusta, Cyprus; and a greater joy came when we were transported to the exotic Golden Sands Camp, a holiday resort for British soldiers in the Middle East. Alas, our stay was to be very short–two days–just enough time to "wet your whistle" once. Back on board ship, we found ourselves heading for Egypt and soon landed at Port Said, where we stayed in a transit camp for another two days. While there, we were to have our first encounter with the Arabs, who were in revolt against their own corrupt king, and agitating to get rid of the British forces from their country.

Our permanent camp was at Genifa, a few miles from the town of Fayid, near the Suez Canal. There we were, living in tents with very little to do and no place to go. Everybody was moaning and groaning, wishing they were home again. Because of the political situation and the terrorist activity, we were confined to camp, and it was one of the most boring times I ever spent in my life.

Then it happened! An announcement was made that we were to be allowed into Fayid for one day's liberty, and there was rejoicing throughout the camp. There were restrictions, of course, just to let us know we were still in the army. Twenty-four hours notice had to be given; we had to go in fours, and we had to carry our rifles or sidearms. Well, now, that wasn't really too bad, was it? In quick time I had a quartet formed, had our names on the list, and we were rarin' to go.

The Grand Hotel, Fayid: an unimposing square block building with a flat roof. There was nothing very grand about it, but it was the place we chose to spend our day of freedom. What were the attractions? Wine, women, and song, so it was fine for us. Skajer, Jackie, Spanky, and I sat there just having a great time until we were told to leave because it was closing time. We were reluctant to leave, because the night was still young, and we didn't want to call it quits.

Outside the bar, Skajer suggested waiting around until the staff locked up for the night, then breaking in and spending the night there in a great, marathon drinking spree. Jackie and Spanky reneged and went their own way, leaving Skajer and I to carry out the break-in plan.

There wasn't a sound to be heard as we made our move to the rear door. Skajer kept watch while I forced the lock on the door with my bayonet. When the door was opened, I beckoned for Skajer to come. We smiled at each other, anticipating the great time we were going to have inside. Just as we were about to enter, we heard him.

"Okay, fellows, freeze . . . turn around slowly with your hands raised."

We turned to look into the boyish face of a soldier from our own regiment. He was from a different company and didn't know us. Nervously, he pointed his rifle at us and said, "I'm going to take you guys to the guardroom."

Although his rifle had a fixed bayonet and a magazine of shells, it wasn't cocked, and I decided to take the only chance I could see to get out of the situation. Quickly I pulled my rifle from my shoulder, put a round up the breach, and, pointing it at the guard, said, "You're not taking us anywhere. You'd better drop that rifle."

The poor fellow just stood there looking at me, not knowing what to do. I was sure he'd turned a few shades paler, losing some of the precious tan he'd gathered in the Egyptian sun, but still held on to the rifle. Well, one thing I learned at school was, "If at first you don't succeed, try, try, again." And I knew it was time to try again.

Placing my finger around the trigger, and with all the determination I could muster, I said, "Now, soldier, I'm going to give you just one more chance; and if you don't drop that rifle, I'm going to drop you where you stand."

"Don't do it, please," he pleaded.

"Drop it!"

"Please . . . !"

As I lifted the rifle to fire, the poor guy looked as if he were going to cry, and he dropped the gun.

"Now turn around," I told him, "and start walking."

"What are you gonna do?" he asked with fear in his eyes.

"If you don't do what you're told, I'm gonna shoot you."

He turned and walked away from us. When he was about 20 yards away, Skajer shouted, "Okay, let's go!"

We turned and ran as fast as we could from the scene, but hadn't gone very far when the soldier picked up his rifle and started shooting after us. We could hear the bullets as they whined over our heads and past our ears, and were happy that the rifleman wasn't on target.

When we arrived back at camp, there was no guard of honor awaiting us, no regimental band playing to welcome us, no flags waving for us. As there had been two soldiers missing, and two soldiers involved in the incident at the

Grand Hotel, the army, being smart, put two and two together and had a cell waiting for us.

A cell? Well, not really! It was a regulation army tent completely surrounded by high, barbed-wire fence. It was a concentration tent, but they called it a cell, and who was I to argue with the army? As we walked into camp, all I could hear was the sound, not of sweet music or cheering, but of our regimental sergeant major bellowing, "Put those two men in the cells!"

"Okay, you two idiots," roared the R.S.M., who followed us into the tent, "I'm going to throw the book at you this time. I'm going to make it my business to put you both away for a long time."

Next morning we were on company orders charged with "Whilst on active service, forcing a safeguard to lay down his arms." Events moved according to the usual army routine: from company orders to commanding officer's orders to district court-martial. And it takes a lot of time to get from one end to the other—six weeks–and that time was spent in the concentration tent. After a lot of red tape and military rigmarole at the court-martial in Fayid, we were both found guilty and sentenced to six months imprisonment.

The military prison and detention barracks on the outskirts of Fayid is just like one of those concentration camps you see in the movies. It was completely surrounded by a high, double-barbed-wire fence. Some of the prisoners were accommodated in a concrete cell block– the "cooler"–and some in tents. The staff, the lowest rank of which was sergeant, had been handpicked for their toughness and ability to enforce discipline. It was no holiday camp.

I thought I'd seen everything evil in my world, but that prison made the corruption and violence in Sandy Row look like a Sunday school picnic. I never thought I'd live to meet, and live with, such a fraternity of degenerates as was in that prison. It was a pit filled with, humanly speaking, the scum of the world.

As in every prison, the prisoners engaged in some smuggling activity. Work parties went out every morning and contraband came in every night, in the form of cigarettes, tobacco, matches, a little hashish, and other things. Every day there was someone caught, but most got by without trouble. Every day I was out I managed to get something in—except once! I was caught bringing in cigarettes and was sent to the cooler for three days on bread and water. But that didn't stop me from smoking— not even in the cooler! And it didn't stop me from smuggling; for as soon as it was safe to do so, I was at it again.

In the prison the men would smoke almost anything; and next to tobacco, it was a common thing to smoke dried tea leaves, sometimes with a mixture of tobacco and hashish, rolled in the very finest of India paper. The poor old army chaplain was so encouraged because so many of the boys were requesting Bibles. Little did he know they were using those precious pages to roll their cigarettes.

By the time we were released from prison, our regiment was moved to Tel-el-kebir, near the town of Ismalia. The camp was a huge ordinance depot in the desert, enclosed by 17 miles of double fencing. The area between the fences was mined, and every mile around the perimeter there was a giant searchlight on a high tower. Every night an ambush guard was dropped a half mile from each searchlight.

All this security didn't keep the Arabs out, for every night they were there to plunder. From time to time we caught them; and occasionally some of them would lose their lives in the mine field or when they were spotted by the searchlight and tried to make their escape. When they were caught, they were usually beaten and questioned before being handed over to the Egyptian police.

We only spent one year in Egypt before returning to

England and Dover Castle. I had only one year to serve to complete my five, but the closer I got to the time of my release, the more I was in trouble. I was charged with wilful defiance of an order, after refusing to double march for the provost sergeant and then for the R.S.M., both of whom were glad to see me locked up for a while.

One of my final confrontations with the R.S.M. happened in downtown Dover. After the bars closed, I was standing in line in the fish-'n'-chips shop, when the R.S.M. and a friend walked in. They had the audacity to walk right to the front of the line. When I reminded them that they should go to the back, the R.S.M. pulled rank on me. Before he knew what was happening, I had him by the scruff of the neck, pulled him into the street, and walloped him. Two military policemen were quickly on the scene and were about to take me into custody, when a group of sailors, who'd seen what'd happened, threatened to dump them in the dock if they touched me. I walked smartly away, got back to camp, and never heard another word about it. But I did keep out of the R.S.M.'s way until it was time to go on leave again.

Back in Belfast, I was walking in Great Victoria Street with a civilian friend when I saw two military policemen approach. I was half-drunk and improperly dressed, not having a hat or belt on while in uniform, so I knew I was in for trouble. As the M.P.'s got close, one of them reached out to grab me, and I punched him in the face, and a fight started. I was fighting with one, and Ernie was fighting with the other. One on one was fine with me, but then a car with four civilian policemen arrived on the scene and spoiled things. They took my friend away, and the M.P.'s handcuffed me and took me to the nearest military barracks, from where I was escorted back to Dover.

Back at the castle I was sentenced to 28 days detention, after which I was called before my commanding officer.

"Gorman," he said, "I'm putting you on probation. If you're in any more trouble within the next three months, you'll be discharged from the service. I'm just about sick, sore, and tired of you and your behaviour."

I didn't tell the guy, but I felt just the same way about him and (in my mind) his crummy regiment. So he thought he was threatening me with something awful. What a laugh! I didn't wait for three months to give him my answer, for as soon as I received my next pay, I was on my way to Belfast—A.W.O.L. I knew I was finished with the army—well, almost!

I never did get back to see my commanding officer, for I stayed in Belfast and had no intentions of going back under my own steam. They were wild days! I fought, drank, mugged, and burglarized until I was caught. Then I was caught on a bum rap. I was innocent of the crime with which I was charged but was too embarrassed to tell the truth.

Sergeant Simpson, you threatened that you'd make a soldier out of me or break me in the process. You were wrong, Sergeant! You failed! My parents tried and couldn't! Who's going to try next? God? That's what Pastor Kelly thought, but he didn't know me—no one can change me!

5

The Queen's Jail

With one hand on the Bible and the other raised to heaven, I promised the court I'd tell the truth, the whole truth, and nothing but the truth; then I promptly perjured myself. Most of what I said in court was a fabrication of lies. I couldn't tell all the truth *that* day! If my mother and the other members of my family hadn't been there, it would've been different. Or if it had been a military court-martial overseas, I would've told the truth; but not in Belfast.

Phil and I were charged with burglarizing the home of a wealthy lady. Although we were not caught on the premises, we were identified by an eyewitness, and picked up by police, 50 yards from where the alleged crime was committed. Even though I wasn't guilty, I wasn't prepared to tell the whole truth.

I'd spent more time in that so-called burglarized house than I had in my own in recent days. The lady, who lived alone, knew me and knew me well, for she'd been my "sugar mammy," supplying me with all the money I needed just for living with her. If I'd told the truth, it could've been proved by the stubs in her cheque book, for my name was on many of them. The problem that night was that I brought a friend, and Helen was angry and ordered us away from the house. When we refused, she called the police. Everything would've been just fine if I'd been alone. Never once during the court proceedings did she acknowledge she knew me, nor I her.

Detective-Constable Alister convinced the magistrate that we were guilty of a crime, and we were remanded on bail, to appear at the high court. My mother posted bail for both of us; but as soon as we stepped outside, we were arrested by the military police. In spite of my mother's pleas, we were taken to Palace Barracks, Holywood.

I was indignant with the army for arresting us after my mother had been made responsible for our appearance in court. But I went calmly and cooperated, determined the army wouldn't hold me very long. Regaining our freedom was more simple than I thought.

If someone told me it happened to them, I wouldn't believe them—it's so incredible! The authorities at Palace Barracks, not wanting to have us on their hands, concluded that we should be held on open arrest at army headquarters in Lisburn, and released us to make our own way there. Needless to say, we'd no intentions of going anywhere near Lisburn or any military establishment. When we failed to show up at headquarters, we were hunted by both civil and military police.

Those four weeks on the run were filled with excitement and fun, as we were pursued by police and almost caught on a number of occasions. One night the police raided the Sandro Cinema while we were there, but the patrons kicked up such a racket that it was easy for us to make our escape. Another time we were in Phil's brother's house when the police arrived at the front door. Like a flash we were out the back door, over the yard wall, and lost to our pursuers in the dimly lit streets of Donegall Road. In the early hours of the morning we were found sleeping on the top deck of a city bus, by a policeman; but he let us go when I showed him some identification and explained that I'd had a hassle with my father and left the house in anger. Then for 10 days we lived in the home of a Christian widow, whose son was a corporal in the military police. She hid us from her own son; and on the day we were to appear in court, she wept, prayed for us, and gave us each a copy of the New Testament.

We did intend making our appearance in court because my mother had posted bail. On entering the building, we saw an army officer with a detachment of military police and knew they were waiting for us. We decided to play a little game with them. As soon as they approacned us, we ran out through the door; they followed, but we slipped in through another door. Ten minutes later they came back, and we were standing waiting for them. The gallant officer completed his conquest by informing us that we were under arrest, and we had the joy of sitting in court with them until our case was called.

In the first case a Belfast butcher was accused of being a member of the IRA and being in possession of a machine gun and a quantity of ammunition. The machine gun was found on top of the cold storage in his store. He was found guilty and sentenced to 18 months in jail. I thought, If he got 18 months for his crime, I should get about 2 for mine, if I'm found guilty.

When they called our case, we were escorted to the dock by two policemen. Having no interest in supporting the legal profession with my ill-gotten gains, I applied for legal aid. But I would've been as well defending myself, for they sent an obtuse army lawyer to defend me. The man wasn't alert to what was happening, or didn't know what to do, so he simply read out my record of army service. Strange defence indeed! It was enough to get a decent fellow hung.

Everybody told a fairly interesting story before the members of the jury retired to consider their verdict. But, alas, they didn't stay out too long, and were soon filing back into the jury box again. None looked our way. In fact, they all looked more guilty than any of the known criminals I'd seen that day. The judge came in and looked their way.

"Ladies and gentlemen of the jury, have you reached your verdict?"

"We have, my lord."

"And what is your verdict?"

"Guilty, my lord."

Judge Porter was not happy with the smile on my face, and it got to him so much that he severely admonished me and was on the verge of losing his judicial dignity. He then tried to remove the grin from my face by sentencing me to 18 months with hard labor. Well, I decided there and then that I was going to grin and bear it.

So it was off to jail we went. That wasn't such a long journey from the court to Her Majesty's Jail which was reached by walking from one side of the street to the other. We didn't even have to go outside, for there was direct access to the prison via underground tunnel. It was while walking along the tunnel that I realized I'd have to chop 2 years off my age in order to stay with Phil in the juvenile section. He was 19 and I was 21. They didn't question me when I lied about my age.

Have you ever been in the juvenile section of any prison? Well, anyone in his right mind probably wouldn't want to be in one, especially in Belfast; at least I didn't. Why? Well, it's early to bed and early to rise—real early! After breakfast and cell cleanup, we were marched to the woodyard, paired off in twos, and spent the morning sawing huge trees with a crosscut saw. Also, twice a week we had afternoon physical education periods.

Another problem was that twice a week we had to go to

school. I was never fond of school, even in prison. But they wanted us to learn "readin', 'ritin', and 'rithmetic"; and as there was no getting out of it, I settled for staying as far away from the teacher as possible. Almost every day I claimed one of the seats on the back row. But as it turned out, I made pretty good progress and finished school before all the others.

Two prisoners were supposed to sit at each desk; but one day three of us rushed for the same desk, and we all made it. The only guy who was sure he had a seat was the one in the middle. Because none of us would move, the officer in charge invited us to the front where there were some nice vacant desks. It was a very gracious invitation which we accepted; and being a gentleman of the highest Irish order, I let my two friends lead the way. I also wanted to observe the welcome they received from the nice officer.

Phil walked up first with a big grin all over his face. The officer soon knocked that off and pushed him into a seat. The second guy had already stopped grinning and was anticipating what was going to happen. It happened! He got the same treatment as Phil. The officer then looked my way.

I approached the officer and was prepared for the blow he aimed at the side of my head; I quickly moved to the right with the punch but immediately bounced back and hit him with my best right. He fell, first on top of the desk, and then to the floor. It was obvious by the expression on his face as he looked up at me that he hadn't been expecting it.

But I didn't wait around to study the expression on his face, keep him down, count him out, or lift him up. I knew that school was over for that day and made for the nearest exit. Outside, I was met by a reception committee of four big, burly officers, who immediately pounced on me. Even though I fought with fists and feet, they just about pummeled me into the ground. They were joined by the officer I'd struck, and he really gave me a belting before throwing me in the cooler, where I was continually harassed and called all sorts of filthy names.

I knew I was in for big trouble, for no one gets away with hitting an officer. Next morning I was a marked man, for the officers began to make my life really nasty. I was marched before the governor, where I learned that the guy I'd hit was also his secretary and friend. Boy, I sure can pick 'em!

"How long have you been in here, Gorman?"

"Four weeks."

"Four weeks, what?"

"Four weeks, sir."

"And already you're charged with insubordination and assaulting an officer. Have you anything to say?"

"Yes, sir."

"Well?"

"It was self-defence—"

"What do you mean, self-defence?"

"I mean, he hit me, and I hit him."

"Do you expect me to believe that one of my officers would strike a man?"

"Well, sir, I think you know what goes on in this place; you know—"

"That's enough, Gorman!"

"But, sir—"

"Shut up!"

"Sir—"

"I've heard enough from you, Gorman. Don't try to get smart with me. I know your kind; you're a born liar, and I'm going to make an example of you. You'll spend three days in solitary confinement on bread and water; one month's dissociation; and you'll lose one day's remission."

I was only in the punishment cell for about five minutes

when I was visited by the goon squad, who roughed me up a little, and a little more when I told them they were marked men. But they knew, and I knew, that I was still the marked man and hated by every officer, because I'd dared to commit the unpardonable sin, according to an unwritten prison law: "Thou shalt not strike a prison officer, for he who does shall never be forgiven—or forgotten!"

Three days seemed to be a long time, especially in a tiny cell with nothing to do. In the cell there's a wooden bed, a table, and a seat, all fitted to the wall. The bedclothes are placed outside the door every morning. On the table there is a Gideon Bible and a Church of Ireland (Anglican) prayer book. I read more of that Bible than I'd read in my whole life before. I also read some of the prayer book to pass the time. But it was pretty boring stuff at that time.

While I was there, they found out I wasn't a juvenile; and on being released from the punishment cell, I was placed in the adult section, which was really to my liking. There was the same old food, but the work was lighter; there was less discipline, and there was no school.

I worked in the mailbag shop at first, then was sent to work in the furnace room. There a civilian instructor trained me to operate two large coal-fired boilers. It was hot, hard work, but I liked it. As soon as I could operate the boilers with a certain degree of proficiency, the poor civilian was fired; for it was known that he'd been smuggling cigarettes and liquor in to the prisoners, and was getting paid on the outside.

On three occasions I was called to the front office, and each time it had something to do with the army. An army captain came to visit me. He was a nice guy, giving me cigarettes, and questioning me about my home, parents, school, work, drinking habits, criminal activities, the army, prison life, and my plans for the future. He didn't tell me what it was all about, and I kept wondering about his visit. I don't know why, but I had the strange feeling he may have been a psychiatrist (or a trick-cyclist, as we called them in the army).

A few weeks later, I was called to the office to see a sergeant from the military police. He really wasn't one of the good guys, but was, rather, very officious.

"Fusilier Gorman," he said, "I am here to inform you that you have been discharged from Her Majesty's Forces. It is my responsibilty to read to you the final assessments of your conduct and character, and ask you to sign it."

He proceeded to read from the discharge book: "The cause of discharge is misconduct. Your military conduct is assessed as being indifferent. Caution: Men who have been discharged from any part of Her Majesty's Forces for misconduct of any sort . . . are cautioned against attempting to reenlist by concealing the circumstances of their discharge. Such reenlistment renders a man liable to imprisonment for two years."

My final contact with the army was when a quartermaster sergeant came to pick up my uniform and left me an old, dyed, navy blue battle dress, and informed me that I owed the War Department £35 for several items of equipment that were missing from my gear. They were glad to be rid of me, and I was happy to see the last of them, even though I was in jail.

In prison a guy simply wants to do his time and get out. Most of the prisoners will tell you that they're going back to a life of crime. Their conversation is inevitably about sex or crime. They'd boast about their biggest robbery, how they fooled the cops, how great they were. Some would share their trade secrets: how to pick locks, blow safes, get guns and ammunition, and get rid of stolen goods, or get a good lawyer. The only thing I didn't hear them talk about was how to get out of jail when you were doing a good long stretch. I personally learned a lot about crime and criminals.

Instead of being an institute of rehabilitation, it was a school of crime.

They even had preachers and church services in prison. There were four official chaplains: Catholic, Church of Ireland, Presbyterian, and Methodist. Since I'd received infant baptism in Sandy Row Methodist Church, they reckoned I was a Methodist. John Wesley may have had a different opinion. The Methodists had their little service every Wednesday, and all the Methodists had to attend. Then, because the Methodists didn't have service on Sunday, they had to go and worship with the Presbyterians. I'd never been in church as much in all my life.

I always looked forward to the chapel services, but not because of the sermon or the singing, neither of which were very bright. On Wednesday it was great getting away from work for that hour; and on both days it was a great opportunity to see friends from other parts of the prison. It was that time when messages were passed back and forth, and there was an exhange for cigarettes, tobacco, matches, tinder, flints, books, and lots of other things. The services didn't have any special spiritual significance; it was just a nice social time!

In my initial interview with the prison chaplain, he was interested in hearing about my past life and especially my travels abroad. I learned that our chaplain in Belize was a personal friend of the prison chaplain. After our little visit, he put his hand on my shoulder and gave me this profound advice: "While you're in here, behave yourself; and when you get out, be a good boy." Good boy? I thought, where did he come from? And where on earth was it possible to be both a good boy and still have a good time? At that period of my life my profound mental answer was, no way, man!

Once they had an evangelistic mission at the prison conducted by an officer in the Church Army (Anglican). There were services every day for a week; and although attendance was optional, the chapel was full every day. Most of the sermons flew over my head and left me wondering what it was all about. But the singing was different than in the usual church services. Most of the prisoners joined in (some using words that weren't in the book). Everybody seemed to enjoy the special singing and music. Each day some of the fellows would stay behind for prayer, but most of us thought they were on some sort of con game. In our cells at night we'd think about what happened in chapel.

Nights are the hardest in prison, for every one of them is long and lonely—especially when you're in a single cell. An awful spirit of dejection swept over me when the cell door slammed shut and I heard the key turning in it.

What does a guy do in a single prison cell? He stares at the steel-covered door and resents being locked up like an animal. He paces up and down and feels bitter. He reads a tattered library book until his eyes get tired reading in the dim light. He feels sorry for himself and succumbs to fits of depression. He counts the painted bricks on the four walls and counts again the number of days until his release. He tries to look through the tiny observation hole in the door, or he climbs to look through the barred window. He listens to the footsteps of the prison guard and estimates where he is. When he knows the officer is not near his cell, he bangs his metal mug on the hot water pipes, knowing that someone somewhere will reply in the same manner, and he'll feel good because he has communicated with some other living person, even in this primitive way.

Other things he does can include some pushups, running on the spot, or shadowboxing, until the officer looks in and tells him he's stupid. He thinks of home, a girl friend, a mother, and he weeps. He thinks of the past, and he dreams and plans for the future. He thinks of what he'd like to do to the guys who put him there, and intense hatred builds up. He talks to himself, and sometimes to a God whom he doesn't know. When the lights go out, he gets out his tinder, flint, and cigarettes he's smuggled in, and has a smoke, blowing the smoke into the ventilator shaft or out the window. He gets into bed and twists and turns until he finally falls asleep.

Time flies, they say, but not in prison! The hands of the prison clock turn slower than any other clock. When you're caged in like an animal, there are more than 24 hours in every day, and there are more than seven days in every week. A month is a long, long time, especially when most of it is spent alone. Those last days are the most difficult, and often it seems they'll never end. Excitement is beginning to rise; it's more difficult to sleep, and the days grow longer still. Then the time comes when you climb into the hard prison bed for the last time, and you say audibly, "I'm getting out tomorrow . . . I'm going home!" And you can feel the hot tears of joy well up in your eyes and run down your cheeks.

The day of freedom has finally come, and you're out of bed earlier than usual. You're so thrilled with the thought of freedom that you can't eat your breakfast, but the fellow in the next cell is glad to have it. You know you're going to see the governor at nine o'clock for the famous farewell lecture, and how you wish you were standing on the other side of that big wall.

Marching into the governor's office, I had the feeling I'd been through all this before. He looked up at me, after I'd been standing there for a minute, and there was a stern look on his face. "Gorman," he said, "your time is up. If you'd behaved yourself, you'd 'ave been out sooner. I hope we've seen the last of you here. When you get out, find yourself a job and keep out of trouble. That's all! Good luck!"

At the reception room where I handed in my prison

clothes, I was expecting to get the old army battle dress. But I was joyously surprised to find my mother had left me a complete new outfit of clothes. It was great just putting them on. I felt free just wearing them, even before I walked from the administration building to the prison gates.

"Well, good-bye for now, Gorman," sneered the guard as he opened the gate. "You'd be as well leaving your things here, for you'll be back soon."

Outside the prison gates I stopped, looked around, breathed in deeply, and it felt good to be alive and free. I only wish that feeling of freedom had lasted a long time. It didn't! In less than an hour I was in the bar drinking with my old cronies. I stayed there all day and was carried home that night. The next morning I woke up wondering where I was, and I was sick.

"God can change your life," reechoed the preacher. What a laugh! Everybody else had failed—my parents, the army, the prison authorities! What did Pastor Kelly think his God could do? If I couldn't change my own life, how could He?

6

The Impossible Dream

The world is full of dreamers, and I'm to be numbered with those who spend some time, whether awake or asleep, in the land of fantasy. Most of my dreams are daydreams, dreams which will hopefully one day become reality. They are aspirations I have for my own life, for my family, for my church, for my world! I believe the dreams I now have are inspired by God.

The other dreams I have are dreams in the night over which I have no control. One of these strange dreams keeps recurring. Even though the people and the places in each dream differ, there is always the same story and the same conclusion. In that dream I'm back in the army, have completed my terms of service, and should be discharged; but the army refuses to release me. I keep trying to see my commanding officer or someone in authority, but I just can't get near them. A sergeant in the orderly room keeps telling me I've still two more years to serve, because every day I spent in the punishment cells has been added to my time. I protest, telling him I've served my time and want out immediately; but he tells me it's impossible, and there's no way I can get out. There the dream ends, leaving me frustrated and defeated.

That is not the only impossible dream I've had in my life. I can't remember a time when I didn't have a dream for my life, even though my actions may have seemed to say something on the contrary. I knew some of the things I wanted to do, but I didn't know how to reach my goals. I know that iron bars don't make a prison, for I was imprisoned in a red-brick jungle from which I couldn't escape. As far as I was concerned, I was imprisoned for life.

I didn't plan to be a perpetual reject: kicked out of a dozen different jobs, out of the army, out of my home, out of society, into jail. But what else was there for me in life? I'm not proud of what I've done, and I really wish that things had been different. I wanted them to be different and tried to make them different. In the army, when my C.O. told me to "turn over a new leaf and change my way of going," I did try! Honestly! I can remember the many times when I tried to stop drinking, to stop gambling, to stop stealing, to go straight; but they all ended up in failure.

Even though I was an outcast—a 100 percent failure—the desire to be different never left me. Like others, in my dreams I wanted to be *someone* in the world. I dreamed of having a decent job which I liked; of meeting a nice girl, falling in love, and getting married; having children of my own; of doing something meaningful to make my own worthwhile contribution to the world. I wanted these dreams to come true.

During my time in prison and immediately after, my dreams seemed to get farther and farther away from me, as if lost in a fog. In fact, there were those times when the

65

dreams were so shattered, I thought they'd never be realized. They were just dreams—impossible dreams! It's easier to dream about work than it is to get it.

And even if I wanted work, where could I get a decent job? Where could I find *any* work? It was tough enough for any person to find a job in Belfast; but if you'd been kicked out of the army and had a prison record, it was just impossible.

I was a good boiler man and could handle the largest coal-fired boilers, and from time to time there were vacancies for which I applied. But even when they were convinced that I could do the work, my answers to these inevitable questions turned them off: Where did you learn your trade? Where did you last work?

I was so disgusted on those occasions I'd just hit the bottle and hit it hard. I stole money so I could drink, and got so hooked on liquor I didn't want to do anything else. I was slipping deeper and deeper into the gutter, and nobody seemed to care. There were times when things were so low I'd buy a bottle of cheap wine, mix it with a bottle of methylated spirits, and have a good cheap drunk.

That was my life! And for guys like me, there's always some way to get a drink. Every morning I'd head for the pub, club, or some drinking joint, and spend the day there. Well, I never knew how long I stayed, for I rarely remembered going home. I'd wake up in the morning, wondering how I'd got home. Then I didn't always wake up at home; but when I did, I'd sneak out of the house—afraid to face my loved ones; afraid of what they'd tell me; afraid of what I'd done; afraid of myself.

I often learned I'd done horrible things while in a drunken blackout: destroyed the furniture and broke the windows in my mother's house; brutally beat my sister until she needed hospital attention; attempted to stab my father with a commando stiletto; called my mother all sorts

66

of filthy names; broke store windows; intimidated and used obscene language to our neighbors. How could I stop such things, or blot out the thought of what I'd done? There was only one way I knew, and that was to hit the bottle and get drunk all over again.

My parents and others kept telling me that I was going to end up in jail again or, worse still, in the mental asylum. I was concerned but was too weak to help myself; and I knew I needed help. Especially when I'd wake up in the middle of the night, shouting and screaming, because of awful dreams. One night I dreamed that I was thirsty and went to the scullery for a drink of water. I remember getting a glass from the cupboard and turning the cold tap. Instead of water coming from the tap, it was a clear jellylike substance, which began to fill the sink and get larger and larger until it filled one side of the scullery, blocking the door. It was then I saw that this great glob of jelly had two eyes—large, watery eyes—and I fought to get out of the scullery; but there was no escape. As it grew, it forced me against the wall, smothering me, and I was sure I was going to die. "I don't want to die!" I screamed. It was then I awoke, fighting and screaming, and trembling with fear.

I was scared! People told me I had the delirium tremens, and they warned me to stop drinking, or see the doctor, or join the A.A. program. I knew I should stop drinking, for it was killing me; but I wasn't going to see any doctor, for I was afraid they'd lock me up. And as I didn't know anything about A.A., I didn't even bother to think about it. But I was so sick and so weak that even though I wanted to stop drinking, there was an inner compulsion driving me to it. I was a slave to the bottle, and that meant trouble.

I began to realize that my days at 53 Eureka Street were numbered, for whenever I saw my parents, there was a big hassle. My father finally got to the place where he hardly ever spoke to me; and when he saw me in the street, he'd cross to the other side to avoid me. The break came one morning when he shook me awake. He was angry and shouted, "Come on, you lazy bum, get up, get out, and find yourself a job. If you don't get work today, get some other place to live. We don't want you here!"

I jumped up, grabbed him by the throat, shook him, cursed him, and was telling him what I thought of him and his house when my mother and two of my brothers ran in and pulled me away. I told them that I didn't need to stay there any longer, for I had lots of friends who'd be glad to have me stay with them. I warned my dad, "You stay out of my sight, or I'll swing for you." It didn't take me long to pack up and get out of there.

When I looked for those friends I thought would have me stay with them, they weren't to be found. Boy, they had all sorts of excuses, and I ended up in the crummiest lodging house in all of Ireland.

The people who owned it called it a model lodging house. The men who lived there usually referred to it as "the model" or "the mansion." I suppose when it was built, at the beginning of the century, it was a mansion to the down-and-out, but it isn't a mansion anymore. It's a dirty, flea-ridden, smelly hovel.

The men in the model are the outcasts of society—thrown to the scrap heap of humanity. There's no cheaper or lower place in Belfast, but all the men are glad there's such a place to live. They aren't all local men; some of them are university graduates who've been dragged into the gutter because they were unable to handle disappointment and failure. Trying to escape it, they turned to drink and drugs, which enslaved them. In their euphoria they'd still boast about what they used to be and where they used to live.

Why did I have to live in that awful place? I can still

remember the unpleasant smell as I stepped in the door, and the odor is in my nostrils even now: the stink of rancid food, stale tobacco smoke, yesterday's cheap wine, urine-stained mattresses, perspiring bodies that hadn't been bathed for weeks; the stench left by someone who'd been guzzling beer, gorging fish-'n'- chips, and had been sick in the dorm corridor.

A walk down that long corridor was like a scene out of Dante's *Inferno* or the Dark Ages. Passing the numerous little eight-by-six-foot, cell-like cubicles, I heard the coughing and spitting of T.B.- and cancer-ridden old men; the singing, cursing, and raving of the drunk and demented; the pleas of those who simply wanted quietness to have a good night's rest; the snoring or heavy breathing of those who slept, dreaming they lived in the filth and squalor of the lodging house, and would wake up to find it were true.

That's where I lived! No, that's where I *existed*, in the lowest possible strata of society. The youngest man in the place, I paid my few shillings every week to have my own little cubicle in one of earth's lowest abodes. One look at the place and its residents made it easy to get away to the nearest bar as quickly as possible . . . away to my dearest friend and worst enemy—alcohol! Yet, when I was in possession of all my faculties, I'd cry out from the depths of my being, "What am I doing in this filthy pit?"

The journey from where I was in the lodging to sobriety and normal living was a long, uphill one. I know, for I started out on that journey so many times, making it partway up, stumbling over some obstacle, and then falling and rolling back past the place where I started. My heart cried out for help to get to the top, but there was no help; and too often I concluded, "I'll never make it; it's just impossible!"

Any kind of life would've been better than the one I was living; even life in prison had been better. There I had friends, good food, and a clean bed. While drunk, these things were going through my mind, and I decided to go back to jail again, via a downtown shoplifting spree in one of Belfast's largest stores. As planned, I was caught, placed under arrest, and locked up in the cells in Chichester Street Police Barracks.

Sometime later I was called to the front office, where the sergeant informed me that my father had bailed me out. My father and I walked across the city to Sandy Row without looking at, or saying a word to, each other. At Eureka Street we parted the same way, and I walked two blocks to a wine store, where I picked up a large bottle of wine. With the bottle concealed in my jacket, I surrendered to the place from which I wanted to escape only hours before. There I sat with thoughts of disgust, drinking cheap wine, until I was transported to an ocean where I swam in waters of oblivion.

On Sunday I wakened with the old "morning after the night before" feeling. Not only was I sick, I was downcast with the aimlessness of my life, and in my heart I wished I were dead. I didn't want to live anymore, for I couldn't see any purpose in my existence. How could a person ever get so mixed up? I looked at my surroundings and wondered again, Why would I want to give up a nice, clean bed and good food for a crummy hole in a two-bit lodging house? A guy's values had to be upside down for him to be so stupid. Another feast of wine brought that day to a close.

On Monday morning I arrived at the court and was met by my father and some other friends who had arranged for a slick lawyer to represent me. Monday morning is always one of the busiest at the magistrate's court as they seek to clear the weekend backlog. There was the usual parade of prostitutes, drunks, vagrants, disturbers of the peace, brawlers, and shoplifters. Hey, that's me!

"How do you plead, Gorman?" asked the magistrate.

"Guilty, Your Honor."

"And what do you have to say for yourself?"

"I was drunk, sir."

"Is that all you have to say?"

"Yes, sir."

"Do you have anyone to speak for you?"

"I am representing the accused, Your Honor," said my lawyer, as he stood up. "As you know, Your Honor," he continued, "Gorman has a criminal record and since being released from prison, has been unable to find work. I know he has tried. But because of his dishonorable discharge from the army and his prison record, no employer wants to hire him. He became discouraged and took to drinking, which caused friction at home, and was asked to leave. Living away from home, in a place frequented by the criminal element of the city, and his addiction to alcohol, led to his appearance in court. My client, Your Honor, is genuinely sorry for his actions and is prepared to make restitution. I would ask you to give him a chance to prove himself and, rather than send him back to prison, place him on a period of probation."

"No restitution is necessary," replied the magistrate, "since all the goods were recovered. Are the accused's parents in court?"

"His father is here, Your Honor."

"Will Mr. Gorman please come forward?"

Out of the corner of my eye I saw my father as he walked forward. He looked worried, twisting his cloth cap in his hands, his face flushed with embarrassment. A policeman had to tell him where to stand, as he'd never been in court before.

"I know this must be discomforting to you, Mr. Gorman," said the magistrate, "but you do want us to do what is best for your boy, don't you?"

"Yes, sir."

"If your son promises this court that he will behave himself and go and find work, will you let him return home?"

"I will, sir."

"Gorman," said the magistrate, addressing me, "will you promise this court that you will behave yourself and go and find work?"

"Yes, Your Honor."

"I want you to move back with your parents and go out today and find work. There's work in this city for those who are willing to work. If you don't find work, you'll soon be back in jail. You know that, don't you?"

"Yes, Your Honor."

"I'm placing you on probation for a period of two years. An officer of the court will check to make sure that you're living at home, behaving yourself, and actively looking for employment. You can go now."

Outside the court, my father and I parted company. We still hadn't spoken to each other. He went to his work at Belfast Corporation Gas Department, and I to move my razor, toothbrush, soap, and towel from the skid row hovel to the Gorman mansion. My mother was obviously elated to have me home again, and wept for joy. It was for her sake that I made up my mind to settle down and do all I could to find work.

After lunch, I went to the Labor Exchange to see if they could help me. It wasn't easy getting from Donegall Road to Exchange Street, for I met at least a half dozen people who invited me in for a drink. I was sorely tempted to go in "just for one," but resisted. Never had I passed so many bars before without going in, especially when I'd so much money. I was amazed at my own determination to go straight, and had a confidence that I never had before, feeling that this time I was going to make it.

I was no stranger to the Labor Exchange, for twice each

week I was there in the line of the unemployed. On Tuesday we'd register, and on Thursday we'd pick up our unemployment benefits. This time I was honestly looking for work. I walked to the counter, taking my unemployment insurance card from my pocket, and wondering what kind of reception I'd get from the guy standing there. Civil servants aren't known for their civility, especially to guys of my calibre. I placed my card on the desk in front of the clerk.

"Can I help you?" he asked.

"I'm looking for a job."

"What kind of job?"

"I'm a boilerman, but I'll take anything."

"Where did you last work?"

"I was in the army."

"When were you discharged?"

"Two years ago."

"Two . . . years . . . ago?"

"Yes."

"What've you been doing?"

"I've been unemployed!"

"As an ex-serviceman, you should've had no trouble getting work."

"Well, I've had trouble, because I was kicked out of the army, and I've been in jail."

"Well, that makes a difference, doesn't it?"

"What difference?"

"Employers don't want to hire ex-cons; it's just as simple as that."

"Then you don't have anything for me?"

"Nothing that's suitable."

"Okay, man, you know what you can . . ." I made some vile comments to him.

"Don't get cheeky with me, Gorman; we get dozens of your kind in here every day, and—"

I didn't let him finish, and what I said to him cannot be repeated here. But when I picked up my card and headed for the door, he knew what I thought of him. No, I didn't head for the nearest bar, although the thought did cross my mind. I was still determined to find work if it were possible, and so I spent the remainder of that day going from place to place. It was the same old story wherever I went: "Sorry, no vacancies."

That evening I was sitting watching television when my father came home from work.

"Did you look for a job?" he asked.

"Aye!" I replied, without looking up.

"Did you find anything?"

"No."

"Where'd you look?"

I told him all the places I'd been to, but it didn't seem to satisfy him, for he was still grumpy.

"Well, there's work to be had if you want it; you'd better try again tomorrow."

"Aye, I will."

There wasn't another word spoken all night. I just sat there feeling sorry for myself and believing all the world was against me. There were tears of self-pity in my eyes, and I didn't really know what to do. Lest I would be drawn to the bar, or something worse, I felt I just had to stay in the house. Sitting before the television, but oblivious of what was on the screen, I smoked cigarette after cigarette, and wondered what I was going to do, and where I was going to go. When I could stand the tension no longer, I went upstairs to bed, where I tossed and turned most of the night.

Sunrise on Tuesday morning saw me up and dressed, and immediately after breakfast I was out to look for work; but all I got that day was exercise and discouragement. I got tired walking and tired listening to guys telling me,

"Sorry . . . You wouldn't be suitable . . . No vacancies . . . We'll take your name and address . . . Come back next week . . . We'll let you know." It all meant the same thing—there're not jobs available for people like me!

I was so dejected I didn't go home for supper. I knew my mother would be grieved and concerned, but I couldn't help feeling the way I did. I knew if I were to go home, there'd be an ugly confrontation with my father, and I didn't want to hack that. Also, I didn't want to go near Sandy Row, where I would meet some of my buddies and finish up in the bar. Heading for the nearest restaurant, I ordered tea, fish-'n'-chips, and bread and butter. I ate without enjoyment. Indulging in another spate of self-pity, I sat there thinking about my life: the past, the present, the future. I thought of those who'd given me impossible counsel.

The prison governor said, "Find yourself a job." In court, the magistrate advised me, "Get out and find yourself work." My father wanted to know, "Did you get work?" Where? How do you get work? What kind of employer is going to take a chance and give a guy like me a job? I tried, I honestly tried, but it was no use. You can't do the impossible, and it was impossible for me to get work. I was convinced that it wasn't going to be possible for me to continue to go straight, no matter how much I wanted, for everything and everyone was against me. I was destined for the gutter! My lot in life was to be the drinking den, the crummy lodging house, the prison cell.

In the restaurant I'd allowed myself to build up a furor of hatred, and so I left in anger. I hated the governor of that prison, detested the magistrate in the courtroom, despised my own father, abhorred those who expected me to do the impossible, and was angry with those employers who needed workers but turned me away because of the past. I had a grudge against society for refusing to give a man another chance, and kicked him so hard when he was down that he could never rise again. I resented and cursed the whole world, and headed for the nearest bar.

On Wednesday morning my father shook me awake, but I didn't want to wake; I didn't want to live! If only I could go on sleeping and never wake again, it would be the best thing that could happen to me, for I didn't want to go into that world again—ever! I was fed up! The night before I'd hated all the world; I still hated it with an intense hatred, but now I loathed myself completely. I heard my father's voice, and it seemed ever so far away; but it was him, and I heard him say, "Come on, boy, you'd better get up now; it's time you were out looking for a job."

I didn't get up, but fell into a deep sleep and began to dream. In that dream I saw those who tormented me. They were standing together: the prison governor, the magistrate, and my father. All were pointing to me and repeating after each other, "Go and get work! Go and get work! Go and get work! Go . . ."

I cried out with all my heart, "I've tried! Honestly! You've got to believe me; I've tried!"

But they wouldn't listen. They just kept pointing those long fingers of accusation and chanting, "Go and get work!"

I must've been shouting in my sleep, for my mother came and wakened me, wanting to know what was wrong. I was wet with perspiration, and trembling, but I told her I was alright. She left the room with tears in her eyes and a concerned look on her face.

Most of the next two days are lost to me. All I remember is going to the bar and drinking—just drinking! On Saturday morning I awakened, not knowing where I'd been or what I'd been doing, and I was afraid. What would my family tell me when I went downstairs? How could I walk past my neighbors? What was the matter with me? Why does life have to be like this?

How I wished that things were different! I'd tried to change my life but was worse now than at any time in the past. That's how it was to be; any change in my life would be for the worse. My parents had tried to help, as had the army and prison authorities, but they all gave up in despair. They concluded that I was beyond help and left me to my fate.

But not the Nazarene pastor! Bert Kelly was at the street corner, telling me again, "Gorman, God can change your life!"

7

Requiem in Belfast

It was a motley crowd that gathered at the street meeting in Sandy Row as the Nazarenes proclaimed their Bible message of deliverance for those who were captives of sin. The meeting closed on a sacrilegious note as the pastor called out the words of the last hymn:

"What can wash away my sin?"

"Try Tide!" shouted a merry-andrew in the crowd, to the amusement of most of the people.

That same night, at eleven o'clock, there was a half night of prayer in the Church of the Nazarene. There were about a dozen people gathered in the prayer room, sitting on four benches which formed a square. Bert Kelly, the pastor, and Clifford Filer, the evangelist, sat together, and all the others looked their way, waiting for them to give direction to get the meeting under way.

Pastor Kelly broke the silence, asking, "Have you anything to share with us, Brother Filer, before we go to prayer?"

"Yes, thank you, Mr. Kelly," replied the evangelist as he stood up. "All day, one verse of Scripture has been running through my mind, and I'm sure the Lord wants me to share this thought with you. Christ is speaking to Peter and tells him, 'Go out where it is deeper, and let down your nets, and you'll catch a lot of fish.' Tonight, we've been out where it is deep, and have seen many people who're living in the depths of sin. We've told them about Jesus and how He can change their lives. Tomorrow, we're going to let down the gospel net for the last time during this revival. Let's pray that God will enable us to catch some real big fish. Let's have faith to believe that God will help us to catch one of the biggest fish that has ever been caught in this area. Remember, God is able to save fully and completely all who come to Him by the Lord Jesus Christ."

Rev. Filer nodded to Pastor Kelly to indicate that he'd finished speaking, and sat down.

"Thank you, Brother Filer. Do any of you have any special requests you'd like to share with us before we kneel to pray?"

"Yes, Pastor," responded Joe, "I'd like you to pray definitely for my cousin, Hughie Gorman. I heard he'd stopped drinking at the beginning of the week, but I saw him coming out of the bar tonight, and it appears he's worse than ever."

"Let's remember to pray for Hugh. I spoke to him tonight, and he's promised to be here tomorrow night."

"Praise God!" said Joe.

"I've been praying for that fellow all week," interjected the evangelist. "He may be one of the big fish the Lord'll give us tomorrow night. Let's believe God for his conversion."

"Amen," responded the pastor. "Let's all go to prayer and touch God for the salvation of Hugh Gorman. Only God can change that young man's life."

With a chorus of "Amens" the group knelt to pray at the benches on which they'd been sitting, and each in turn prayed fervently. They prayed into the early hours of Sunday morning.

Although I rememberd the street meeting of the night before and my promise to attend the Sunday evening revival service, I had no intentions of keeping that promise. After all, what good could it do me going to church? It hadn't done me any good in the past. And, really now, I wasn't altogether a heathen, was I? Why, I'd gone to Sunday school and church most of my life!

I knew enough about church that I didn't want it to be part of my life-style. It's not that I didn't want God, but I'd come to the conclusion that God didn't want anything to do with a scoundrel like Hugh Gorman. I was away out of His league, and there was no way of getting into it, no matter what the preacher said.

Pastor Kelly said he'd send someone to call for me at 6:45; so just before six o'clock I left the house. I was standing at the Clock Bar with some of my friends when my brother Tom joined us about seven o'clock.

"Hey, Hughie," he said, with a big grin all over his face, "someone called at the house to see if you were going to church."

All of the other fellows thought that was a great joke and started to laugh and bug me.

"When did you start going to church?" one asked.

"Are you going to be one of those good-livin' people?" asked another.

"Yes, he's going to be a holy roller instead of an unholy terror!"

"Say, if you get old-time religion, you won't want to mix with awful sinners like us, will you?"

"You know, Hughie," added my brother, laughing, "that person who called for you was a girl, a big blonde with a Bible packed under her wing."

That was enough to generate hilarious laughter from all the guys and was a little more than I could take.

"Ah, shut your mouth," I shouted and walked away.

I headed for home, still not wanting to go to church, but in no mood to listen to those guys bugging me. I didn't know why I was walking home; I should've gone the other way, for I didn't really want to spend the evening at home with my father. But still I went home, thinking I could have an early night in bed.

I'd just closed the door and was hanging my jacket on the nail behind the door, when someone knocked as if they had sponge knuckles. Opening the door, I found the "big blonde with a Bible packed under her wing" standing there.

"Pastor Kelly asked me to call to see if you were coming to church," she said softly.

I just looked at her, gulped, and smiled as I thought of what the boys had said about her. She was really a nice-looking girl, I thought, as I continued to look at her. Then she began to show her nervousness and blushed.

"Are you coming to church?" she asked, a little louder.

I didn't know what to say; for I didn't really want to go to church, but I didn't want to disappoint the girl by saying no.

"Okay, I'll go," I told her.

"Oh, that's wonderful!" she replied, with a little more enthusiasm.

My preconceived ideas of the church were literally shattered as I walked into the Donegall Road Church of the Nazarene. In the foyer I was greeted by a man I'd known all my life. He had a friendly smile and a warm handshake; and as he placed a hymnbook in my hand, saying, "It's great to have you here tonight, Hughie," I knew somehow he meant it!

On entering the sanctuary, the congregation were singing "There Is a Green Hill Far Away," and the singing was such as I'd never heard in any other service. They just weren't mumbling through the song; they were really singing, and there was such beautiful harmony. Glancing around, I was surprised to find that I knew many of the people there. There were neighbors, school friends, and others I knew; so I wasn't among strangers.

The sanctuary was the least "churchy" of any I'd been in, but it had a dignified simplicity that made one feel they were in the house of God. The place was just about filled to capacity, and I thought I'd have to stand in the back, which would have suited me fine. But an usher beckoned me to follow him, and led me to a seat three rows from the front and right in at the wall. It was too close to the preacher for comfort, and sitting there I'd the feeling that every eye in the service was upon me.

When I did look up, I saw there were two ministers on the platform. I recognized one as the man who spoke to me at the street meeting; but I didn't know the other. Both of them wore clerical collars but didn't wear preaching gowns like all the other preachers I'd seen in churches. I preferred them without the robes. I suppose it brought them down to street level, making them more like men, and less like lords chief justice.

While listening to the pastor, I learned that it was Palm Sunday. What that meant I didn't know, but by the way he spoke, I concluded that it must've been an important day on the Christian calendar. After making some announcements and receiving the offering, the pastor introduced a man by the name of Sammy to sing.

Sammy stood up to sing, and I recognized him. He was known to all who frequented the bars in Sandy Row, for he was the leader of many of the barroom singsongs. He was also very fond of the bottle. But here he was, singing in church, dressed to kill, and sober as a judge. I can still remember the song he sang as tears ran down his cheeks:

> *It was His love for me,*
> *That nailed Him to the tree,*

To die in agony,
For all my sin;
For my own guilt and blame,
The great Redeemer came,
Willing to bear the shame
Of all my sin.
Oh, what a Saviour is mine!
In Him God's mercies combine,
His love can never decline,
And He loves me.

Sammy sang with deep emotional feeling, so unlike his rendering of the bawdy songs I'd heard in the bars. His song that night touched a spot in my heart and moved me more than I'd ever been moved before. It appeared to me that the singer meant every word he was singing, and what he sang was real to him. He hadn't always been like that, and I began to ask myself some questions: When did he become like that? How did it happen? Were all the people in the church, apart from me, like Sammy? Was the change I saw in Sammy's life what the minister was referring to when he told me, "Gorman, God can change your life"?

After Sammy sat down, Pastor Kelly introduced the evangelist, Rev. Clifford Filer, who stood up to preach. He was a rugged mountain of a man with a strong Welsh accent. And how he could preach! Up to that time I'd never heard any person preach like he did. I had the uneasy feeling that he was continually looking at me, pointing at me, and preaching at no one but me. And it was no weak, flowery preaching to win the affections of the crowd. The man knew what he was talking about—he knew my heart; and what he had to say packed a dynamic punch, which kept hitting me as I'd never before been hit.

Mr. Filer was preaching about the death of Christ on Calvary, pointing out that this was God's way of revealing

His great love for mankind. He was telling me that there was a Man who loved me so much that He was willing to, and did, give His life as a sacrifice for me. He said if I responded to that love, it would transform my entire life, and I'd be a new person.

I'd never heard that in my life before. Yes, I'd heard about Jesus dying for the sins of the whole world; but that He died on Mount Calvary because He loved Hugh Gorman—that was a new revelation to me. And if there was anything I needed, and wanted, it was love. You see, in my life I felt unloved and unwanted. I felt that my father had no love for me; he wouldn't even speak to me, except in a hassle. I knew that the people in Eureka Street had very little love for me and were telling their sons and daughters, "You'd better keep away from that fellow Hughie Gorman, or you're going to find yourself in trouble or in jail." It seemed to me that the only person who showed any kind of love for me was my mother, and I spurned that love.

Yet, here was the evangelist telling me that Jesus loved me enough to die in my place; and not only that, he told me that Jesus had a plan for my life. In my heart I wanted that love; I wanted to know His plan for my life; and I reasoned, If Jesus really loved me *that* much, surely I ought to do something in return. But what could I ever do for such a wonderful person as Jesus? I honestly didn't know what I could do.

But as the preacher brought his message to a close, he left me in no doubt as to what I should do. I had to confess my sins to God, ask Him to forgive me, accept His forgiveness, receive new life as a free gift from God, invite Jesus to be my personal Lord and Saviour. It was all received through prayer and by faith.

The evangelist earnestly urged the congregation to be obedient to God and turn their lives over to Christ. He then announced the last hymn, "When I Survey the Wondrous

Cross"; and before singing the last verse, he read the words:

> Were the whole realm of nature mine,
> That were a present far too small.
> Love so amazing, so divine,
> Demands my soul, my life, my all.

"Please don't sing these words if you don't mean them," counselled the evangelist. "It would be wrong to sing a lie to God. If you are earnest, sing them with all your heart; and as you sing, commit your life to Christ and start a new life tonight."

In my heart there was a positive response, and to myself, I said, "I'm gonna try this." As I stood there, I made my commitment to Christ in my own crude way, turning my back upon sin and my old way of life. I let Christ know that I was sick of it, sorry for it, and asked Him to forgive me. I didn't understand it all, but I invited Him to come in and dwell in my heart, and be my personal Saviour. Praise God, in that moment He did!

Before I responded to the appeal made by Clifford Filer, or raised my hand for prayer, or went to the inquiry room, the work was done! I knew it; I was different . . . I was a new person! The pastor didn't have to tell me, neither did the evangelist; for as I stood there, the blessed Holy Spirit was telling me. He was giving me the unmistakable witness that the work was done, and telling me that I was born again.

It felt so wonderful! At that time I didn't know all the terminology or the language of Canaan, but I had the experience. I knew what the old Scotsman meant when he testified, "Aye, laddie, it's better felt than telt." It was a 20th-century miracle! What my parents had been unable to do; what the British Army had tried so hard to do; what prison authorities could never do in a million years; and what I concluded was impossible, Jesus Christ was able to do in a moment of time. "He is able also to save them to the uttermost that come unto God by him" (Heb. 7:25). Praise God!

When the evangelist did make the evangelistic appeal, I raised my hand requesting prayer, and later went to the inquiry room. Some people were wondering why I went to the inquiry room smiling, while others were going crying. Mr. Filer came to speak with me, asking me to kneel with him by one of the old rickety benches, where they'd prayed for me the night before.

"Well, Hugh, what're you asking the Lord to do for you?" asked the preacher.

"He's done it!"

"He's done what?"

"He's changed my life."

"When?"

"When I was standing out there in the church, singing the last song."

"Well, praise the Lord!" exlaimed the evangelist. "And that's what you'll have to do, Hugh. Right now, just praise God for what He's done for you!"

"How?"

"Just say, 'Thank You, Jesus, for what You've done for me.' "

"I don't know if I can. I've never prayed that way before."

"Don't worry about that, son, God isn't looking for any big, eloquent prayer. Just tell Him how you feel, in your own words and in your own way. He'll understand and be happy with you."

"Dear Jesus," I prayed, "thank You for what You've done for me. You know I've never prayed like this before, and I don't know if I'm even using the right words, but this man says You'll understand. You know as well as I do that something wonderful happened to me tonight. You have done for me what no other person could. Nobody in this world wanted to give me an even break, but You have. I need You, Lord, so don't ever leave me, or I'm going to make a real mess of things again. I'm going to need You around to pick me up when I fall . . . Thanks, Lord."

"Listen, Hugh," said Mr. Filer, "Christ is with you now, and He'll be with you all the time, if you want Him. But you must do your part. Let me show you what has happened to you tonight."

The evangelist opened his Bible and pointed to a verse of Scripture, saying, "Read that verse for me, Hugh."

" 'But as many as received him, to them gave he power to become the sons of God, even to them that believe on his name' " (John 1:12).

"What have you become tonight, Hugh?"

"A son of God?"

"Right! Now, read this verse."

" 'He that hath the Son hath life; and he that hath not the Son of God hath not life' " (1 John 5:12).

"Read the verse before that."

" 'And this is the record, that God hath given to us eternal life, and this life is in his Son' " (1 John 5:11).

"Good. Now, tell me, Hugh, what have you received from God?"

"Eternal life?"

"That's right! Look, Hugh, I've a little saying written in the front of my Bible; would you like to read it?"

"Sure. 'God said it—in His Word; I believe it—in my heart; and that settles it—forever.' "

"Do you understand what that means, Hugh?"

"It means that nobody can undo what God has done for me tonight."

"That's it! If you keep true to Jesus, you never need to lose the assurance and joy you have right now. You never want to lose it, do you, Hugh?"

"No, sir."

"Hugh, here are some things which are important if you are to grow as a Christian: start attending church regularly; read your Bible and pray every day; tell other people what Jesus has done for you; and get involved in the work of the church where you want to serve the Lord."

After Rev. Filer prayed with me, Pastor Kelly and some of the other people welcomed me into my new family—the family of God!

On leaving the church, I walked for about two hours, thinking about what had happened to me. When I arrived home, everyone was in bed; but a coal fire burned brightly in the hearth, and everything was so peaceful that I decided to sit by the fire for a while. As I sat down, my hand went to my pocket for my cigarettes. I took one from the packet and was about to light it when the Holy Spirit spoke to my heart, "You're a Christian now; you'll never need to smoke again." That was enough for me; there was no struggle, no craving, as I took the cigarette from my mouth, and the packet from my pocket, and threw them all in the fire. It was a real liberating experience to watch those tiny sticks of weed, which had enslaved me for years, go up in flames. Somehow I knew that God had already started to work in my life, and He was with me at that moment, and I was enjoying His presence.

Even though my eyes were closed, I could still see the flickering of the flames; and I knew the fire was still glowing cheerfully, for its warmth reached every part of my body as I knelt before it. I was conscious that all the warmth I felt didn't come from the fire, for there was a newfound warmth within that could come only from His presence—it was Jesus! There I experienced what the two disciples experienced on the road to Emmaus, when their hearts burned within. It was the same burning sensation that John Wesley referred to when his heart was strangely warmed on the night of his conversion.

His presence—the presence of Jesus—made that time a feast I enjoyed. There I met the real and living Jesus. I felt that if I'd opened my eyes, I'd have seen Him; or if I'd stretched forth my hand, I'd have touched Him; it was just so satisfying to know He was there. It was the first time I'd been alone with God, and I felt like Peter on the mountaintop—I could've stayed there forever!

"Dear Jesus," I prayed, as tears of love and appreciation trickled down my cheeks, "thank You for these past few hours; they've been so precious. If this is a forecast of what life is going to be like, it's going to be great! I don't know about tomorrow, but I'm glad You do, and I leave it with You. I need You. I need Your help!"

As I climbed the stairs to my bedroom, I knew that life inside my tattooed skin was different; and for the first time in my life I felt I was really alive and going somewhere. Stretching out peacefully on the bed and closing my eyes, I looked back and saw the old Hugh Gorman. What I saw wasn't a very pretty sight, for the man I saw was a slave to the world, the flesh, the devil. But I knew that that person— the old Hugh Gorman—was dead! The rebel had passed away, and the revival from which I'd come had been his requiem—a requiem for a rebel!

Falling asleep, I had no fears of tomorrow, for God had changed my life.

8

Reborn to New Life

"God has really changed my life," I whispered, as I sat up in bed on Monday morning, for the joy of the new life was still very real, and I felt good. There was no craving for a cigarette or for a drink, and I remembered what had happened the night before, and was unafraid. For the first time in years I wasn't ashamed to face my parents in the morning. Things were surely different in my life.

Then I looked around the room and realized that even though I'd been miraculously transformed, things around me were still the same. There were still the same cracks in the ceiling; the plaster was still being held to the wall by the wallpaper; the roof was still leaking, for the wall above the door was wet, and the room was damp.

My environment was still the same, for I was still living in the slums of Belfast. My past criminal record was still on the books. Yes, I was still an ex-con without a job. But the Spirit of the living God wouldn't allow me to dwell on these negative thoughts; and I was reminded that since the previous night, there were some things that were totally different. I was no longer the old Hugh Gorman, for my life had been turned completely around. I was no longer alone, for Christ was with me and had promised to be with me to the end of the ages. I was no longer unloved and unwanted, for Christ had revealed himself to me in love and brought me into a new love relationship within His great family. I was now accepted in and by the Beloved. And, whereas my past was still the same, my whole future destiny had completely changed. That's what Christ did for my life!

I lay for a long time thinking about what I'd do that day, knowing that I'd have to go and look again for work. I also knew that I'd have to tell my parents about my conversion, and wondered how they'd receive it. I was going to need help, and the Lord would have to be by my side, for I couldn't make it alone.

Just as I was about to go downstairs, the Holy Spirit reminded me that I hadn't read the Bible or prayed. As there were lots of Bibles in our home, I got one, read some verses from John's Gospel, and prayed that God would guide me that day.

Downstairs, I found my mother preparing breakfast. As soon as she saw me, tears welled up in her eyes, and she came and threw her arms around me. "We all heard what happened to you last night," she exclaimed, sobbing. "We'll help you all we can, son." And together we wept for joy.

That's the way it was wherever I went that day. People would stop me in the street and tell me they'd heard the good news of my conversion. The word had spread around the district like wildfire. Many of my old buddies were skeptical, of course, and assured me it wouldn't last.

"We know others who tried it," they told me. "We'll give you a week. . . . You'll never be able to pass the bar. . . . You'll be drunk before church on Sunday. . . . You're after that blonde. . . . You're on a con game. . . . You're going to rob the church."

When I arrived home that night, my father was sitting at home. Our eyes met, and as I looked into my dad's face, I cried; for in that moment I realized how much trouble and heartbreak I'd caused him. His eyes were wet as he said, "I'm glad, son!"

Being a Christian didn't give me any special privileges with the world's employers. It didn't mean I was going to get a super job with easy money. I still walked from place to place trying to find work, but there wasn't any to be found. People still didn't want to hire an ex-con, whether he was a Christian or not.

One day I was cleaning the church; God spoke to my heart about looking for work. He asked me if I were really trusting Him to help me find a job. Kneeling at the altar, I prayed, "Lord, I know You want me to work. Maybe I've slipped up somewhere and haven't gone where You've wanted me to go. Lead me, this day, to the job You want me to have, and I'll do whatever You want me to do. Please help me, Lord."

Rising from my knees, I felt better, and was sure that things were going to work out. I'd been trying too hard in my own strength, thinking too much of myself and my past record, and not really depending on the Lord. Now, to be sure it was of God, I wasn't going to look for work until He put His thumb in my back and said, "This is the place!"

That same day, I was coming from the Ormeau Avenue Public Baths and passing the administration offices of the Belfast Corporation Cleansing Department when I heard God speak to me. "Well, this is the place! You haven't tried to get work here, have you?"

"No, Lord."

"Well, why don't you go in and tell them you're looking for work?"

"Are You sure, Lord?"

"Yes, I'm sure!"

"But, Lord, You know the kind of jobs they have there: brushing the streets, cleaning public latrines, emptying sloppy old garbage cans. It's dirty work!"

"I know."

"That's not really a nice job for a Christian, is it, Lord?"

"Didn't you say you'd do anything for Me?"

"Yes, I did, Lord."

"Will you do this for Me?"

"Yes, I will, Lord. I'll go."

Well, I went in with some reluctance, and what d'you know? They had a job for me, and I was to start the following morning. I was there on time at the Tate's Avenue depot, where they gave me a hugh brush and set me to work sweeping the Lisburn Road. I did this kind of work for a week and then—no, I didn't give it up; they moved me to another job. I don't know if it was promotion or not, but I didn't get any extra wages when they moved me to a garbage pickup team in the posh Malone Road area of the city. But garbage is garbage no matter where you pick it up.

Many people thought I should've been doing something better than that, but I knew God had made it possible for me to get the job, and I was doing it for Him. I learned that God has His children doing all sorts of tasks: cleaning the streets as well as legislating in the halls of parliament. And because it was God's job for me, it was the best place to be, and I wouldn't have traded places with the president of the Bank of England. What wonderful opportunities I had to live and witness for Jesus. I had the joy of seeing many of my workmates coming in under the sound of the gospel, and seeing some of their lives transformed by Christ. From time to time I was offered other employment, but I was too happy doing the work that God wanted me to do, and I wasn't going to move until He moved me.

From the very beginning of my Christian life, I started taking an active part in the work of the church, and was serving the Lord in many different ways. On the Saturday following my conversion, I was with the group conducting the street meeting in Sandy Row. It was with fear and trembling that I stepped into the ring and gave my testimony for Christ for the very first time. All day I had dreaded the thought of having to do it, for I was afraid that I wouldn't be able to express myself well enough to be understood. It was the devil telling me that! But my help came from the Lord! People who wouldn't normally stop at a street meeting, stopped when they saw and heard me, and God spoke to their hearts. At that street meeting, in the weeks that followed, I had the joy of seeing men and women transformed by the power of God.

I'm glad that back there, God gave me a love—an insatiable hunger—for His Word. I carried my little Bible wherever I went, and read it at every available opportunity. Because of the lack of privacy at home, I'd often go to the park and sit there for hours just reading, and memorizing, the Word. Some of the verses I memorized back there are the most precious to me even today.

One day, after I'd read the Bible, I was especially praying for the people of Sandy Row, and God challenged my heart.

"You're thinking of all your friends in Sandy Row, aren't you?"

"Yes, Lord."

"You know, all of the people in the bars in Sandy Row are going to be lost unless someone goes and tells them of My love."

"I know, Lord."

"I want you to go and tell them. Every Saturday when those bars are crowded, will you go and be My witness?"

"Oh . . . Lord!"

"Will you go for Me?"

"Yes, Lord, I'll go."

What a challenge! It was a difficult assignment, and one with which I wrestled, even after telling the Lord I'd go. I knew I couldn't do it in my own strength. If I was going to go into those bars and face those people, the Lord would have to go with me. I knew He would, but I was still very apprehensive.

There are about a dozen bars in Sandy Row, and on Saturday night there's never any shortage of customers, as well-earned (and some not so well-earned) money pours into the coffers of the bar owners. From the time God spoke to me, I visited those bars every week and witnessed to the people of the mighty power of God that can transform lives. It wasn't easy! The first night, I walked into one of the bars and gave a tract to the barman. He immediately rolled it up and hit me right between the eyes with it. For a moment I felt like jumping over the bar and ramming the thing down his throat, but the Lord restrained me. I just looked at the barman, gave him another tract, and said, "John, I'd like you to take this tract and read it when you get time."

"Okay, Hughie, I will," he replied, adding, "I'm sorry; I shouldn't have done that."

"Forget it, John!"

That was just one of the many interesting things that happened in those bars, in which there was never a dull moment. On other occasions I was challenged to fight, to sing a song, to tell how I'd stopped drinking, to pray for them, to visit them in their homes, to visit their loved ones in the hospital. In those homes and in the hospitals, I saw the hand of God at work, transforming lives and healing bodies, through believing prayer.

Nancy was one of the people I was asked to visit in the hospital. She was a neighbor who'd lived in Eureka Street all her life and, like myself, had been an outcast—unwanted and unloved. From her teens she'd been a prostitute. Many times, as a boy, I'd go to the wine store and pick up her liquor for her and her boyfriends, and she'd always pay me well. In later years I'd see her in different bars, and always she'd offer me a drink. I liked Nancy, as a friend, and could identify with her because she was despised by the other residents of the street.

I looked at her as she lay in the hospital bed, wracked with pain and riddled with disease. Her name was on the critical list, and she wasn't expected to live more than a couple of days. Her eyes were closed.

"Hello, Nancy," I almost whispered.

Her eyes opened and she smiled. "Hughie Gorman! What's this I've been hearing about you?"

"What've you been hearing, Nancy?"

"Oh, I heard that you'd turned to good livin'."

"It's more than good livin', Nancy; Jesus has completely transformed my life."

"I'm glad to hear it, Hughie," she said, with tears in her eyes. "I never expected to see you up here. You visiting someone?"

"I came to visit you, Nancy."

"Well, I don't know what you want to visit the likes of me for."

"I thought we were friends, Nancy. That's why I'm here. I heard you were ill."

"I suppose. Oh, Hughie, I know I'm never going to get out of this place. You've been in jail, and I've been in jail, so we both know what it's like; while you're in there the time just drags; but you know that one day they'll swing that gate open and let you out. It's different in here; I'm a lifer—never going to get out of this place alive; it's the end of the line for me!" And she sobbed.

"Nancy, it doesn't need to be the end; it can be the beginning."

"The beginning of what?"

"The beginning of an exciting new life with One who really loves you."

"Love?" She laughed sarcastically. "How could anyone

ever love the likes of me, Hughie? Men have wanted my body and have been willing to pay for it, but none of them ever loved me."

"Nancy, will you let me read something for you?"

"If you want."

"And the scribes and Pharisees brought unto him a woman taken in adultery . . . They say unto him [Jesus], Master, this woman was taken in adultery, in the very act. Now, Moses in the law commanded us, that such should be stoned: but what sayest thou? . . . He lifted up himself, and said unto them, He that is without sin among you, let him first cast a stone at her. . . . And they . . . went out one by one . . . and Jesus was left alone, and the woman standing in the midst. . . . He said unto her, Woman, where are those thine accusers? hath no man condemned thee? She said, No man, Lord. And Jesus said unto her, Neither do I condemn thee: go, and sin no more" (John 8:3-5, 7, 9-11).

The tears in Nancy's eyes were now finding their way down each side of her face to the clean, white pillow.

"Nancy, that woman was no better than you or I. Jesus didn't condemn her. Neither does He condemn you. Policemen have accused you, and magistrates have condemned you, but Jesus won't. He loves you and wants to forgive and help you."

"You really think so?"

"I know so! My life was no better than yours, and in many ways it was worse; but Jesus forgave me and helped me to begin a new life. He wants to do the same for you. Would you like Him to do it, Nancy?"

"Yes, I would . . . I really would!"

As we both wept, I'd the joy of helping Nancy commit her life to Jesus Christ, and in a moment of time her whole countenance was changed, as Jesus gave her peace and assurance. Two days later she went to be with Jesus.

The Donegall Road Church of the Nazarene was not the

place for Sunday-go-to-meeting Christians, for there was something on almost every night, and there were six regular worship and service activities every Sunday. Each activity was meaningful and made a spiritual contribution to the spiritual life of the community. In that church a praying people produced such a spiritual atmosphere in which people were saved, healed, filled with the Spirit, and called to full-time Christian service.

It was in the Monday night missionary prayer meeting that I had an unusual, but unforgettable, confrontation with God. We were praying that God would raise up young men and women to take the message of the gospel to the uttermost parts of the earth. There seemed to be a special burden for the Republic of Ireland, our neighbors to the south, where there was practically no evangelical witness. As I prayed, God drew strangely near and began to commune with me.

"Lord," I prayed, "raise up young people in this city who will go and tell the people in the south of Ireland about Your Son and His wonderful plan of salvation."

"What about you? Will you go?" the challenge came with unexpected impact. To that moment I'd never given any thought to such a prospect. Even when Pastor Kelly suggested that one day I might be a Nazarene missionary in the Cape Verde Islands, I dismissed it with a laugh. But now I was hearing the voice of God, and He was expecting an answer.

"Me, Lord?"

"Yes, you, Hugh."

"But, Lord, look at me, I'm a nobody—a garbage collector!"

"I know who and what you are; but I also know what you can and will become. Will you go?"

"But, Lord, I'm a nothing person who can hardly put two sentences together without stumbling."

"I want you to be a minister of the gospel."

"Me, a minister? How can I be, Lord? I don't have the education, or the money. I don't even know if I can get into college; and if I do get in, I don't know if I can make it."

"Have I ever failed you in the past, Hugh?"

"No, Lord."

"I've been your Helper; I will see you through. Will you go?"

"Yes, Lord, I'll go."

I've learned that if God calls you to some task, He'll also prepare you for the task. Things that you could never do naturally, the grace of God can enable you to do. If we trust Him, Jesus gives us the strength to do the things we have to do.

Having said yes to the call of God, I now had to make preparations. I applied and was accepted as a student at Hurlet Nazarene College, near Glasgow, Scotland, and was given permission to commence in the January term. That gave me just about two months to prepare.

By that time I had a new pastor, Rev. Bill Claydon, who suggested that I start putting some money in the bank every week to save for my fees. A bank? Now, that was something new for me, for none of my acquaintances ever had money in the bank. Banks, I thought, were for rich people; and if guys like me went in, they'd think we were in to rob the place. But I decided to start an account in the Belfast Savings Bank, which seemed to be more in my line.

I needn't have worried about banks, for I never did get my savings account started. On Saturday morning when I was going to make my first deposit, I was having my morning devotions; following Bible reading and prayer, I was kneeling in prayerful meditation when I heard God speak.

"Do you remember the money you stole from Meg Thornton?"

"Yes, Lord, but that was a long time ago."

99

"You never did pay her back, did you?"

"No, Lord."

"Well, as a witness to what I've done in your life, I want you to pay her back today."

"But, Lord, this money I have is for my college fees, and You want me to go to college, don't You?"

"I want you to go to college, but I also want you to make restitution to Meg Thornton, today."

"Today? Saturday? The place'll be packed with customers, Lord."

"Will you do it, today?"

"Yes, Lord, but You'll have to help me."

Meg Thornton was a chain-smoking alcoholic who owned a fruit and vegetable store in Donegall Road. It was the kind of store where all the produce was on display outside in the street. I didn't want to approach the store while there were customers around, so I walked up and down the street past the store until Meg was alone. Then I walked in.

"Why, Hughie Gorman!" Meg grinned, while a cigarette hung from her lips. "The last time I saw you near my store, you were a young hoodlum stealing apples. Now you're a big hoodlum, wha'd'ya want?"

"Meg, as a kid I stole a lot of things from outside your store; not only apples, but pears, peaches, oranges, and even some of those delicious freshly cooked beets. But, Meg, I've done something worse than that."

"Wha'd'ya mean?"

"You may not remember it, Meg, but one night I was sitting beside you in the Wee House Bar. You were really sloshed, and I went through your purse and took every dollar you had."

"No," said Meg, "I don't remember it; but it's not the first time that happened to me; but it's the first time anybody has ever come to say, 'Meg, I stole your money.' "

"Since that time, Meg, I've become a Christian, and the Lord has reminded me of what I've done. He wants me to repay you."

Meg was flabbergasted! She'd never heard of anything like that in her life. Well, neither had I, but I sure felt good when I had done it. It was a good day for Meg, too; for not only did she receive some unexpected money, but she heard about the love of Jesus and how He could change people's lives.

The following week, God again reminded me of something I'd entirely forgotten. Maybe it was a coincidence, for it happened as I was on my way to the savings bank. I shouldn't have been surprised, but I was, as God spoke.

"Do you know Morrison's store in Sandy Row?"

"Yes, Lord."

"Do you remember robbing the store?"

"Well . . . I do now, Lord."

"Do you know what I want you to do?"

"Yes, Lord, You want me to go and pay for those goods."

"Right! Will you do it?"

"I will, Lord."

That's the way it was until it was time to go to college; and as the weeks went by, I was happy to make things right with people whom I'd wronged. I was so glad to do it for Jesus, because He'd done so much for me. Well, what's money, anyhow? It's what I needed to get into Hurlet Nazarene College! Did I ever worry about the money I needed for college? Of course I did! But not for long, for most of the time I was confident that the God who called me to preach, and led me to make restitution, would supply all of my needs.

I was more concerned about things other than money. Because of my lack of education, I was determined to study as much as possible before going to college. English grammar was a must for me, so I took a course with Wolsey

101

Hall, Oxford, which helped me tremendously (believe it or not). I also ploughed through the introduction and first volume of Wiley's *Christian Theology*, with the help of my pastor, Bill Claydon. But more than anything, I read and studied the Bible.

Two weeks before leaving for college, I gave notice to my employers that I was quitting. At that time I wondered how the Lord was going to supply my need. I knew it wouldn't drop out of the blue sky, but how was God going to do it? I had some of the required texts, a *Thompson Chain Reference Study Bible*, and my passage booked on the Belfast-Glasgow steamer. But as yet I didn't have my college fees, which had to be paid in advance. Only the Lord and I knew that I didn't have the money, but only the Lord knew where it was coming from.

During my last day at work, the boys were kidding me about leaving a good job to become a schoolboy again, and we were having a good laugh together. I was kind of sad to be leaving the fellows whom I'd grown to love and appreciate. That evening, as we were preparing to go home, the foreman called me.

"Hugh," he said, "we've all appreciated having you on the team and are going to miss you. We're all proud to see one of our fellows go away to college to prepare for the kind of work you'll be doing. We all want to have a part in it—here's a little something from the boys."

There were tears in his eyes as he made the presentation, and tears in my eyes as I received it, for that gift would mean more to me than those fellows could ever imagine. I was so grateful to them for what they'd done; but the tears in my eyes were also tears of thankfulness to God, for I knew this was His way of supplying my need to go to college.

I was so excited and couldn't get home quickly enough to open the envelope; and, glory to God, there was just enough in it to pay for my first year's tuition and board at the college. That was all I needed! God had been true to His promise.

God was with me from my first day in college, and He knew I was totally dependent upon Him, perhaps more than any of the other students. I was one of the oldest students; most of them were just out of high school, and I'd been away from school and study books for about 10 years. I needed all the grace that God could give me in those early days at college. The students had a good laugh when they heard me speak with my hard, nasal, west Belfast accent. And they laughed when I told them I was a garbage collector before coming to college. Bill Henson, one of the tutors, commented, "Well, Hugh, where there's muck, there's money." That brought another round of hilarious laughter in the lecture hall. But those guys stopped laughing when I tackled the biggest student in the college—in fun, of course! Praise God, I made it all the way to graduation, received my preacher's license, and was ordained to the sacred ministry. Some people told me I'd never make it! I couldn't have done it alone, but then I wasn't alone, was I? Jesus led me all the way!

In college, I met Joan, a student from Cape Town, South Africa, who is now my wife and co-worker in the ministry of making Christ known. The Lord has been pleased to send into our lives two fine boys, Wesley and Timothy. These three very precious people are God's very special gifts to me, and they have brought much joy to my life. There are still times, even now, when I have to stand back in amazement, observe all that God has done for me and given me, and exclaim, "Is this for real? Has all this really happened to me?" And knowing the reality of it, I just pour out my praise to Jesus, for He has done all things well!

Since that day when I met Jesus in Belfast, my life has been one great adventure. I've been adventuring with

Jesus! He and I have travelled together, spreading the good news of full and free salvation. We've been thrilled to see souls respond to the claims of the gospel in every corner of my beloved Ireland . . . in England . . . in bonnie Scotland . . . in the great Dominion of Canada . . . and from coast to coast in the United States of America. What a privilege has been mine to tell people of all ages, in different countries, "God can change your life!"

. . . This is what I told them that day I went to preach at the prison crusade meeting. That day I sowed the good seed of the Word of God in tears, and had the joy of reaping in ecstasy, as five young men yielded themselves to Jesus Christ and found real freedom for the first time. I was glad that I'd gone and sat where they sat, and had the joy of sharing my Jesus with them; for they are now my brothers in earth's greatest family. And one day I will rejoice with them in heaven.

The dark shadows of that penal institution gave way to the brightness outside as I walked from the prison. It was a beautiful summer's day, and the sun was shining, and the birds were singing; they too were happy and free. I walked down Crumlin Road with a spring in my step, a song in my heart, and praise on my lips. There was Someone beside me, and I spontaneously expressed myself to Him by saying, "Thank You, Jesus! It's great to be free! Yes, it's great to be free indeed!"